BORN to BREAK the BOUNDARIES

Stacey Santonastasso

BORN TO BREAK THE BOUNDARIES

Lizzette Balsdon - The Editing Queen and friend for life.

Jenna Matz - JAM Design & Media, Book cover.

Meghan Egnatowicz - A.M.E. Photography

DISCLAIMER

This work depicts actual events in the life of the author as truthfully as recollection permits and /or can be verified by research. This book is, first and foremost, a memoir. It reflects the author's present recollections of experiences over time. Occasionally, dialogue consistent with the character or nature of the person speaking has been supplemented. All persons within are actual individuals; there are no composite characters. Some events have been compressed, some dialogue has been recreated. Some dates, places, events and details may have been changed, invented, and altered for literary effect. The reader should not consider this book anything other than a work of literature. All characters and incidents and dialogue are real, and written as memories of the events described in this book and maybe different to fill in gaps as best she could.

Dedication

To anyone who has the honor of raising a child.

Table of Contents

Preface

My son is Nick Santonastasso, CEO of his own company, fitness and runway model, body builder, motivational speaker, author and YouTuber. It's a privilege to have a son who is so successful, but what is even more extraordinary, is the fact that Nick was only given a 30% chance of surviving birth. He was diagnosed with Hanhart Syndrome – an extremely rare genetic disorder that left him without legs and only one arm, which ends in one finger.

Of course, we had no idea how to raise a child with different abilities. We decided that we would do everything in our power to provide this child with our best. And we decided – if he survived birth – to raise him exactly as we did his siblings.

On May 20, 1996, Nick defied the odds by being born. Since then, he has grown breaking through boundaries, and lives life on his own terms.

In this book, I share anecdotes from Nick's life to inspire you, dear reader, to refuse to let your limitations hold you back from achieving your greatest potential. If I could bring inspiration to just one person dealing with a devastating diagnosis, I would be honored.

I'd like to thank Nick for the inspiration to write this book, and my husband who has been with me every step of the way. Thank you to my children who stood by us through the years, and who loved their brother so fiercely.

And last, but not least, thank you, dear reader for picking up this book.

Foreword

It is commonly held that first impressions are hard to overcome. Nick Santonastasso makes an indelible first impression – pure optimism, infectious enthusiasm, intellectual curiosity, and self-deprecating humor – a personality that fills any room he enters. Nick draws people to him – people want to be in his company. His father, Michael puts it simply, "He's just a happy guy."

It wasn't supposed to be this way for the baby born with a rare condition depriving him of legs and inhibiting the full development of his arms. That's not the way it was described by the well-intended medical professionals as they prepared his parents, Michael and Stacey, for the news that their fourth child's prognosis for survival wasn't good. And if he survived, his profound disabilities would be so limiting as to render him dependent on care from others for what was sure to be a shortened life span. What the learned professionals could not have predicted was the powerful role that the love and resilience of an extended family would play as Nick overcame seemingly insurmountable odds.

Nick's mother, Stacey, has written a compelling account of his and the Santonastasso family's journey – beginning before his birth through his school years to his current personal and professional successes. Stacey's story is genuine and unpretentious in the telling. It is a story of parents whose boundless love manifested in their unabashed faith in their son's ability to do anything despite his physical differences from others. Stacey's and Michael's advocacy for Nick took many forms with many people: strangers, doctors, teachers, other parents. Their faith in the Almighty and their determination that no limits be placed on their son lay the path for him to thrive and live BIG. Girded by his parents' love and encouragement, and his siblings including him in their normal play, Nick sought and conquered challenges that many "able-bodied" people decline to engage. He merely adapts challenges to his will, succeeds, and seeks more.

In addition to conveying a heartwarming account of a family's devotion, "Born to Break the Boundaries" contains life lessons for all us to mine as we face our own daily travails and recognize we each have the power to thrive if we believe.

Mary Santonastasso Hagerty
Consultant, University of Maryland College Park
Retired Senior Executive, National Science Foundation

STACEY SANTONASTASSO

The book you are about to read is true, it actually happened. It happened to Michael and Stacey and their son Nicholas. I found about this remarkable story after I re-connected on Facebook with a childhood friend; I never knew that I would learn so many lessons from the life he and his wife lived, but, more importantly, from the son that they raised.

I work with many young people trapped in addiction and it seems like they have everything going for them. Why won't they just stop? That answer is more complicated than what meets the eye, but they are seemingly completely normal. Outward appearances' seeming normal isn't what Michael and Stacey faced after the birth of their fourth child. Nick was born missing both legs, with only one arm which ended in one finger. What they did next, and how they raised their son, would define them and their entire family for the rest of their lives.

From the journey Stacey and Michael and their son Nick have lived, and from my own upbringing, I know how families love their children. But with the Santonastasso's example I can see how it differs from the adult children that I see with addictions. Stacey and Michael raised Nick as a normal child like they have raised the rest of their children. The never taught Nick to be a victim and never told him that the world owed him anything or that he should be treated differently for being born without most of his limbs.

I only wish Stacey and Mike could have read this book when Nick was a baby. But Stacey wrote this, and they really had to figure it out as they went. No matter what your child's situation is, always raise them to work towards independence. The only enabling is to give them the tools they need to succeed and do not do for them what they can do for themselves. Be their biggest cheerlead and always lead with love and faith.

Debbie Strand
Ebb Tide, Regional Marketing Representative, Radio Host at Sober in the City, Certified Recovery Coach, Marketing and PR at Spark Music and PR

As you go through life there are milestones we hope to attain, graduation from school, love marriage and then the birth of a child. We often take those important things for granted or expect they will just happen. We realize very quickly that they don't just happen, each steppingstone has its own challenges, highs, and lows but we push through them because that's what life is all about, isn't it?

It's not until you have the opportunity to have your own children that your perspective changes forever. We are forever a parent, nurturing, educating and protecting them through all the trials and tribulations they must endure. Different from when we were going through these challenges, this is not just what life is about anymore, it is your child's life, it's a special journey that you take with them and we are responsible for them, aren't we?

When you read this book, you understand how the best of the best, Stacey and Mike Santonastasso, have allowed Nick to make a beautiful, independent life, as the title says, Born to Break the Boundaries. They have shown how to take a parents greatest fear, the possibility that your child will be less than perfect and turned it into a story of accomplishment and unconditional love. They allowed their family to know that boundaries is just a word in the dictionary. You can accomplish anything if you have the love and support of your family, friends and the community, can't we?

Nick Santonastasso is an amazing young man with an unmatched drive to be what he was meant to be. The Best, just like his parents and family. The depth of his family influence was best said by Nick himself, "What makes a family strong is Deep-rooted love", that strength and love has carried them through this journey. A journey that is pretty special, wouldn't you say?

Thank you for allowing me to read and enjoy this part of your life. Anyone who has a child will benefit from your story, allowing your child to be who they want to be.

Ruthanne Scaturro
Commissioner, Ocean County Library

BORN to BREAK the BOUNDARIES
How we raised our adaptive child in a handicap world

My son is Nick Santonastasso; Keynote Speaker, Fitness Model, Sponsored Athlete, Bodybuilder, and CEO of his own company— RAW METTLE---, Author, and owner of his own branded clothing line, The Lotus Line. A former prankster and still an influencer, Nick is an amazing person with an explosive personality and a million-dollar smile. A social media sensation with over a million followers on Vine, nearing a half a million on Instagram and Facebook, and has a variety of viral videos on YouTube, Nick has been featured in magazines, on television shows, and speaking venues. He is a world traveler and philanthropist.

CHAPTER ONE

Yeah! I am now pregnant with our fourth child. He is due in May. We will then have 11-year-old Marisa, 8-year-old Mike, and 4-year-old Meghan. My kids are truly excited, especially my son Mike, who absolutely must have a baby brother. He is adamant that his brother's name will be Nicholas. Great name—nothing to change; Nicholas it is.

The ultrasound technician points towards the screen; "This is the heart; these are the lungs; this is the face." He leans forward, squinting at the screen and repeats "This is the heart; these are the lungs; this is the face." My husband, Michael asks, "You don't see the legs?" The technician replies softly "No, I don't see legs. There are no legs".

We're sent for a high resolution ultrasound. I'm on an exam table in a dark room. The only light comes from the big screen on the wall showing images of our baby. There are at least ten other people there, including doctors and medical students.

16

Michael holds my hand and gives it a quick squeeze; he sees the tears rolling down my cheeks while I silently sob. Medical terms are being whispered and I can only catch a little of what they are saying. My bladder is painfully full as the wand on my belly continues to prod around for what feels like the hundredth time. I want to scream that I have had enough.

Finally, the ultrasound ends, and we are escorted out of the room into the hallway while the doctors discuss the results. I do get to use the restroom and—thank God that I did not have an accident.

The door to a conference room opens about twenty-five minutes later, and we are invited in. The doctors are seated around a large table. I look around at their faces and see their grim expressions; now I am super nervous. My heart is pounding in my chest and I feel as though I can't breathe.

"Well, Mr. and Mrs. Santonastasso, we have ruled out Amniotic bands. The cause is unclear to us. Physically, there are no legs. We can only detect one arm, and we can't see the other. Internally, it may have heart, lung, and kidney defects, defects of the reproductive organs, mental retardation, and gastrointestinal disorders, no genitalia, cleft palate, and it may atrophy in the womb."

I hear every word they say, but what destroys me the most in that moment was their reference to "it"—they called my baby an "it".

The conversation continues describing what medical equipment may be needed if "it" survives; ventilating machine, feeding tube. The prognosis is troubling, and we are left with the feeling that our baby is going to die.

Michael and I jump up from the table. We desperately need to leave the room quickly, and I don't know who was dragging whom as we ran out of the hospital as fast as possible.

We drive home in utter shock and disbelief. Michael has a white knuckled grip on the steering wheel and it seems as though he is trying hard to concentrate on driving. I am shaking. My thoughts are running wild and I do not know what to say, so I just stare out the window as more tears fall. After a long silence, Michael turns his head my way and says, "We have to brace ourselves for what could happen".

I was not sure whether we'd be able to bring a baby home, and whether I would be capable of caring for him if we did. I knew nothing about medical equipment, especially if it was going to be connected to my baby. My mind couldn't wrap around what the doctors told me; it is unfathomable…

The little sleep I got during those weeks had me waking up in a panic, and then the hysterics started.

Michael likes to prepare for situations. He tells me all the time that "piss poor planning prevents piss poor performance". I don't even know what to prepare for, I'm so very lost.

We have explained to our parents and a few very close friends the truth of our predicament. Other folks were told that there are complications with the pregnancy, and no explanation was given. My children never suspected that anything was amiss. I would not allow the situation to affect them when it was so unclear what was going to happen. If they asked why I was crying, we told them I was emotional from the pregnancy.

I could not function properly and had to leave my job at the pre-school where I worked. Michael spoke with my boss and was truthful about our situation. At a later date, I heard from a friend that a coworker said I had lied and just wanted attention. Hearing this was extremely hurtful. I had plenty of attention at home.

Thinking back on a few days before, I was in the middle of taking a shower as one of my children continued banging on the bathroom door.

"What do you want?"

"When are you getting out? I'm hungry!"

"Isn't daddy down stairs?"

"Yeah but I don't want to bother him".

"Oh, how nice of you! Ask him to make you something to eat or wait till I'm finished".

Clearly, I'm pretty popular and have a little more attention than I need.

I had to call the women from Bible Study and let them know I was having complications with my pregnancy and could no longer host the group at my home. Of course, they were concerned and asked me for the details. I replied that I couldn't tell them, because in my mind there was no way they could pray for me positively. How could I possibly say "Please pray the doctors are wrong and my baby has arms and legs that his organs are fine, and he's not going to die on me?" One of the moms from our bible study stopped by the house with bags of baby clothes for me.

Shaking my head no, I politely told her I wouldn't be needing them. Her eyes widened and she started to cry. I quickly dispelled her theory that the baby was already dead, we hugged each other, and I told her I can't explain right now.

I sat on the garage floor, surrounded by twisted and broken chaos. Devastating grief overwhelmed me and I launched the baby swing, high chair, and playpen across the garage. Anything baby-related received my fury.

I am a Christian woman, deeply rooted in my faith, but this unbelieving situation has me begging, pleading, screaming, and cursing God. (I know, I won't get to sing in the heavenly choir and I really, really want to). I was in a constant conversation with God—in my head, and sometimes when alone, I would shout out very loudly to him, just in case. I wanted to make sure my prayers were heard. I even had the audacity to tell him he could not understand the depths of a mother's love for her child. OOOOPS

CHAPTER TWO

Nicholas was born on May 20, 1996. He weighed 3 lbs. 14 ounces, and was 12 inches—do I dare say—long). I had a C-section and was crying and scared to death. I kept repeating over and over that I was scared. I was sure that it was too soon for the cut and I was going to feel everything! But a few moments later, I hear him cry. "Oh, my God! He's crying!" I say. Now I am crying harder, because if he is crying he's alive;

Michael watches as the doctor raises the baby and hands him to a nurse. She cuts the umbilical cord, cleans him up slightly, swaddles him in a blanket, and carries our little bundle away before I get to see him.

All of a sudden, excruciating pain flares in my chest. I'm now yelling to Michael that my chest is burning and is on fire. I tell him I'm having a heart attack and I'm dying. My mind is telling me that it is just my heart breaking.

They administer medication and warmth spreads through me. The pain is lessening and I'm fading out, into a deep sleep.

My parents are anxiously waiting outside the nursery. They see a nurse rush by with a little bundle clutched tightly to her chest, and they know its Nicholas. About a half hour later, the pediatrician approaches them and asks if they are the grandparents to baby Santonastasso, to which my mom replies affirmatively.

"Would you like to meet your grandson?"

My mother nods enthusiastically and they are led into a little room by the nursery. The doctor asks her if she would like to hold him. My mother now has bragging rights; she was the first to hold Nick. Fast forward to his adulthood, whenever my mom or dad spoke about Nick, the conversation always ends with "I held him first".

Michael does not leave my side until I'm put in a room. He is going to the nursery, and on the way he prepares himself for what he's about to see—which I'm glad to say is a far cry from the mutation the doctors had described from the ultrasound.

The nurses were gathered in a corner, whispering to each other when they see Michael approach. He told them who he was and they brought him to Nicholas, who was in his bassinet among the other infants. Michael later told me, "I picked him up and saw his beautiful face and I told him he

23

would be okay, that I would take care of him until I die or he did, whichever came first".

He held him in his arms for a long time, bonding and whispering reassurances of how much he loved him. It was getting late, so he put Nick back in the nursery. A torrent of emotions overwhelmed him, forcing him to run outside. He did not want anyone to see him cry. He returned to check on me, sat there for a while, then left to go home".

A week later, I am home from the hospital and my mother-in-law tells me that on the night of Nick's birth Michael arrived home about 11:00 in the evening; she was walking toward our family room to talk to him. My in laws live in an addition that's attached to our home and were taking care of our three other children. She said the room was dark, so she assumed he had gone upstairs to bed, but in the next second she heard my husband's blood curdling scream at the top of his lungs. She said it was so loud, it shook the house and she was certain the neighbors could hear it. I believe after staying strong for all of us for so long the relief that Nicholas is healthy and only physically challenged had my husband reaching his limit and this was his breaking point.

I am in a private room further away from the other mothers. I'm not sure if this was planned or coincidence, but the room number ends with 13 (really!). It's morning now and Michael wakes me. I have not met Nicholas yet. I'm still pretty loopy from a lot of pain medication – okay, I'm super loopy and the C-sections hurts like a mother.

"I'll be right back, I'm going to get the baby," Michael says. I grab his arm and tell him I'm nervous and scared, he says, "Stay [my nickname], he's beautiful", and then he leaves the room. A few minutes later, he wheels in Nicholas who is wide awake, having just been fed and changed.

Michael picks up Nick and places him on the bed; he unwraps him from the blanket, and plucks the little hat from his head. I am in awe. I don't know what I was expecting, but this little bundle is amazing; he is so beautiful! Michael wraps Nick back up in the blanket and places him in my arms, exactly where he's meant to be.

I'm kissing him all over his little face; bright beautiful eyes stare back at me. I fall so in love with this baby and can't stop telling him how much I love him.

Nick is healthy, all of his organs are perfectly normal and working on their own; no cleft palate, and he does in fact have genitals. He is missing legs, his left arm ends with one finger, his right arm ends just below the shoulder. But that is not the first thing you see; what captures your attention is his little face. He is absolutely the most beautiful baby – yes, I know all parents think their children are the most beautiful. Nick has a full head of dark hair and angel kisses on the back of his neck and a very light one on his forehead. I believe the Angels had a hard time letting him go and showered him with kisses and Jesus ever so gently kissed his forehead and whispered his love for him in his little ear.

The next afternoon, our three kids are herded to the hospital room by Michael's parents. They are so excited to meet their baby brother. Michael unwraps Nick from his blanket; he is fast asleep in the bassinet. Three little heads are competing to get a look at him, and then you hear an angel's choir, "Oh my God, he's sooooooo cute!

They are touching him, each trying to kiss him and not one word about missing legs, so as parents, we point out the obvious. My older son turns around and says, "That's okay, he can have my legs". I know—grab the tissues. Hope is entering the picture; our kids are so loving and accepting. They are simply ecstatic to have a new baby brother.

CHAPTER THREE

My heart ached for my son. Mike was so excited that he was a big brother, that, the next day, he began to tell his friends on the bus ride to school all about Nicholas. The bus driver—who happens to be well acquainted with my family— heard Mike's description of his brother.

My husband receives a phone call from the school asking him to come down to the office because they have Mike in with the Principal. Meanwhile, my son has no idea why he's "in trouble". The Principal explains to my husband what the bus driver heard and was very concerned that Mike is suffering from jealousy and attention issues—you have got to be kidding me! Attention issues? Very doubtful. My kids will get right in your face if they feel you are not listening or paying attention to them. Michael proceeds to tell the Principal our situation with Nicholas. He asks for their understanding and support of the staff to ensure our kids have no further issues within the school.

We now have to care for a special needs child—how do we do this? The first child is like a tester; you buy and read the books, go to classes, and you have those great suggestions cards from your baby shower—and let's not forget, your own parents. In time, you figure it out. So, with child number two and then three, you believe you have a pretty good handle on this. Shower them with lots of love and attention, teach them right from wrong, ABC's, 123's, please and thank you and very importantly—NEVER make fun of anyone, don't be mean, and two wrongs don't make a right.

I believe **all** children are special, and some just have special needs. It's a serendipitous thought but I always think that if God entrusted us with Nicholas, he must realize we would raise this child exactly the way we raised our other three.

Once I'm home, there are necessary calls to be placed. I have to get Nicholas a social security card and have him registered with DDD (Division of Developmental Disabilities) I also have been assigned a case manager through DYFS; she is a fountain of knowledge and strengthens me emotionally. She explains to us that if Nick is a ward of the state, he would be provided with all medical equipment, prosthetics, wheelchairs, and developmental care that will have astronomical costs—more than we could ever afford. So basically, if we give him up, he gets everything, and if we keep him, he'll have less.

28

No friggin way! This is not the option we are choosing. We are his parents and will do whatever is necessary to provide him anything and everything he needs. Thank God, our caseworker exceedingly agrees that we are more than capable to fulfill Nick's essential needs; she continues to explain there is access to agencies that provide community-based programs for services and support. She excitedly describes the Early Head Start program for infants (6 weeks old) and toddlers under the age of three, which promotes the physical, cognitive, social, and emotional development of infants, and toddlers through a safe and developmentally enriching environment.

Having a newborn even after three children is challenging, and with Nick it is more so. Trying to keep him dry in a diaper is impossible. Every time he pees, it would leak out the leg holes and soak him from top to bottom. Scotch Tape—new best friend! We tape the holes closed and it stops the leaks. Onesies are a must! I learned that lesson when I put Nick in just a T- shirt and diaper; he wiggled around so much that the diaper slipped right off.

Bathing a baby is tricky at the best of times. Bathing Nicholas has risks. Thankfully, he fits perfectly in the bathette I placed in the kitchen sink, but babies are very slippery. I know I have to keep a death grip on him, because if he slides down the tub I am afraid he will drown. Add some soap and you have got yourself a super slippery situation, but Nicholas

29

loves his bath time. Now, how to get him out the tub; wrap him up in a baby towel? I am worried I will drop him—just kidding; I got this!

CHAPTER FOUR

Life in the Santonastasso household is nonstop activity and organized chaos. And let us not forget the mom taxis and carpooling. My oldest, Marisa, is at gymnastics practice and I need to pick her up. Mike is at his friend's and I have to collect him on the way. Meghan is patiently waiting in the car, watching me trying to get my act together. I now have to put this tiny baby in a car seat. I'm terrified if I turn the corner, the center strap will slide and he'll slip out the bottom. I start cramming blankets around the bottom of the car seat to fill the holes where legs go; it works perfectly. Now I have to dig through the blankets to find that damn slot the chest strap locks in. I am sweating, my back is breaking from hunching over, and I am late to pick up my daughter; but hey, the baby is safely snug in his car seat. I figured out quickly that anything with leg holes needs a blanket shoved in them. Baby swing, activities centers, and bouncy seats.

Our case manager suggested I speak with other parents of children who have special needs. I spoke with several moms whose children had a variety of afflictions. They did offer information about medical and daily care, what they **had** to do for them. In essence, Nicholas would not be able to accomplish anything on his own. I was absolutely disturbed by this and told Michael about the conversations. I vowed that **never** again would I listen to advice given by parents; however, I would be more than willing to offer any of my own experiences but did not want to hear any preconceived notions of what my child could or could not accomplish. This may seem harsh and I sound bitter, but I've had so many negative opinions in the last few weeks I believe it's best to handle one situation at a time.

Nicholas was six weeks old when we took him to the Alfred I DuPont Hospital in Delaware where we met with a geneticist for an evaluation. It was there that we confirmed the name for his condition: Oromandibular Limb Hypogenesis Syndrome or Hanhart Syndrome. Somewhere between the 56th and 59th day of a baby's development, something goes awry—nothing we did or did not do is the cause. Infants who have this condition can suffer from a spectrum of disorders that include lack of limbs, heart and kidney defects, defects of the reproductive organs, mental retardation and gastrointestinal disorders. This condition occurs one out of 500,000 births. Experts say the cause is unknown and only twelve children have been born with this syndrome—most died in utero, because such babies often have a deformed heart, lung and digestive systems.

We are handed an eight-page evaluation, but what stood out the most was the prediction that Nick would probably spend most of his life in a wheelchair. By now, our emotions have been stretched beyond the norm and the last couple of months have been difficult, but overall, we considered ourselves blessed since this situation could have been so much worse. We are keeping a positive attitude despite what we have been told. We are truly happy and have kept a sense of humor.

Michael and I brought Nick with us to my six-week checkup. He lay in his baby seat on the floor in front of us in the waiting room. A pregnant woman looked up from her magazine to look at our baby. It was totally normal for her to look, and she couldn't seem to take her eyes off of Nick as realization set in. She went back to her magazine, and it is clear that what she saw has shaken her up a bit. The woman continued to look from the magazine to Nick and then back to the magazine, for a few more minutes until the door to the waiting room opened. A nurse appeared and called my name. As we stood up to enter the doctor's office, Michael looked over his shoulder and saw the pregnant woman looking at him with questions in her eyes. He smiled at her and said, "Forceps". He waited a beat and added, "Just kidding!" He turned his head back around and walked through the door. You might be thinking that was cruel, but our kooky sense of humor seems to be an outlet for our pain.

CHAPTER FIVE

Our family is seated on the first row of bleachers while Nick is sleeping in his stroller next to me. Some parents we know congratulated us on our new baby, as we settled in to watch my son, Mike's baseball game. After several games in the season their team has won. The boys are in high spirits. The coach informs the team that he will treat them to ice cream at our town's favorite dairy stand. Mike ran over and told us he is going with his teammate and close friend; the mother offered to take them to the dairy stand and back to his friend's house to hang out. About an hour after we returned home, Mike's friend's mother calls for me to pick him up. I pulled into their driveway just as the mother came out of her house, located two streets over from ours.

I had met her a few times and she is usually friendly, but not this time. By the look on her face, she is very upset. I wondered if the boys got themselves in trouble or possibly had a fight. I got out of the car to meet her halfway as she walked toward me. She then flat out told me that Mike was no longer welcomed at her house; I thought it was because of his behavior and prepared to apologize. Her next comment caught me off guard. She glared at me and said that, in her culture, I must have committed a heinous crime to have had a child born with deformities.

I could not believe what I was hearing. I turned towards her open front door and yelled "Mike lets go, now!" and by the tone of my voice he knew I was serious. He came running out of the house and jumped in the car. I took a few more steps and got in her face and said "Lady, I don't know who your God is, but **mine** is loving and forgiving. He would never punish me or my child for a sin you **think** I committed".

I got back in my car, looked at her and said, "I really feel sorry for you and your culture not knowing what it's like to be loved by **your** God". As I drove back to our house, I looked over at Mike. I did not know what to say to him. I knew he heard the whole conversation. He was lost in thought, staring out the side window. He suddenly turned to look at me with a smirk on his face and said, "She's a dope!"

I smiled back at him—I am not even going to tell him, "That's not nice".

CHAPTER SIX

Nicholas was three months old when we attended a family celebration for my cousin, and not all relatives attending the event are aware of Nick's condition. I had him dressed in the most adorable sleeper outfit, and tied the legs in a knot at Nick's bottom so the empty legs do not dangle—it was a definite fashion statement.

I was holding Nick, who fitted in the crook of my elbow to my palm. My mother's much older aunt approached to see the baby. She was gushing on and on about how beautiful he was and then asked me if maybe he was uncomfortable having his legs bound. I just kind of looked at her funny and told her "He doesn't have any. He was born without legs. He also has one arm and the other is a stump just below his shoulder."

I watched her face turn pale, and she started to visibly shake. I was totally uncomfortable waiting for her response. After she took a few moments to compose herself, she gave me a huge hug with tears in her eyes and said, ""I'm so glad you didn't put him in an institution". This was not the reaction I expected. I was actually appalled! I could not understand why she would say such a thing. I walked away telling her over my shoulder that I needed to find my mother.

My mom was talking with her cousins; and I rudely interrupted the conversation by telling her I needed to talk to her right away. I grabbed her arm and walked her to the other side of the room where no one could hear me. Through clenched teeth I growled out, "Mom, your aunt just said she's glad I didn't put Nicholas in an institution. Why the hell would she say that to me?"

My mom thought on this a moment, and explained that her aunt's granddaughter was born with Down syndrome, and her daughter put the baby in an institution. It broke her heart, because her daughter would not let her take the baby; the whole situation was kept very hush. I did not know what to think or say. My mother added that, back then, babies born with abnormalities were not accepted in society, so they would put them in institutions.   Yeah, I'm not touching this one.

Later that evening, after all the kids were sleeping, Michael and I were relaxing with a cup of coffee. I began to tell him about the incident with my mother's aunt and told him what my mom said to me. Michael said, "No way in hell are we going to hide our kid. I want everyone to know about him and I'm going to make sure they do".

38

The day after, Michael placed a call to the mayor of our town and explained our situation. He invited her to our home to meet Nicholas. I was a little nervous about meeting her— not because of Nick, but because she's the Mayor!

The doorbell rang. I answered, expecting her to be dressed in a suit, looking very formal; but standing before me is a woman a little taller than my five feet, outfitted in a duck yellow raincoat, duck yellow rain boots to her knees, and a floppy rain hat. I wanted to laugh, because her appearance immediately put me at ease and she graced me with a most friendly smile. Once I started speaking with her, I found her to be the most lovely, compassionate woman ever!

Here is what she wrote in the Township Newsletter.

Baby Nicholas—he's a few months old. A beautiful [told you] dark-haired, bright-eyed, smiling baby boy. Round and sweet, any family would be proud to have this precious bundle. Surrounded by the love of his siblings, Marisa, Mike, and Meghan, and his adoring Mom and Dad, baby Nicholas is indeed a contented, secure child.

Sadly, for reasons unknown to us, this lovely baby was born without legs and one arm is a stump below the shoulder. The other arm is normal, but has a hand with only one finger. In all other ways, this little boy in a blue blanket is normal. What will the future bring? Years of unending therapy. A lifetime of prosthesis. Years of special accommodations for baby Nicholas.

Yes, Nicholas Santonastasso has a family, and they love him with all their hearts. He is theirs, but they are ours. They are our neighbors, our friends, our schoolmates. We shop with them, attend church together, and share a community. They need our love for reassurance; our prayers for support—and yes, our financial help. They cannot do this alone.

As you watch your own little ones running and playing, think of baby Nicholas. As your youngsters perform the most mundane daily activities, remember the baby who will always have to go the extra mile to be part of the group.

Let's reach out and enfold this young family. We live in a beautiful township and seem to have every material comfort. Let's show that we also have compassion and love for our neighbors who need us. Please dig deeply into your hearts and pockets, and contribute to the Little Nicholas Medical Trust Fund.

My child will now have what we hoped and prayed for; to be accepted as the wonderful, warm and happy little boy that he is. That's all—just to be accepted.

Our Community did embrace us with the outpouring of affection and concern; many generous gifts were given to the Little Nicholas Medical Trust Fund. Local lodges, organizations, church groups, neighbors, and friends held fundraisers. Spaghetti dinners, pancake breakfasts, dances, auctions, fashion shows, softball tournaments, and a walkathon enabled us to purchase Nicolas his much-needed medical equipment. So many volunteers gave their time, treasure, and talent to make all the events a success and their efforts and loving support was sincerely appreciated.

CHAPTER SEVEN

Nick received a lot of public attention and is a little local celebrity, but that does not stop the stares we receive in public.

One morning, our family went out for breakfast. We were seated at a round table and we put Nick in a booster seat. Marisa, Mike, and Meghan sat in the chairs across from us. The kids were looking at the menu and chatting about what they planned to order.

I gave Nick his crayons to color on the kid's menu. Yes, Nick had his own crayons—they have a round top with hole he sticks his finger in that come to a point at the end, like a regular crayon.

The waitress took our order and the kids were talking to Nick, asking him what he was coloring. It's at this point that Nick decides to fling the crayon across the table which he finds very amusing and starts laughing and waving his arm in the air. This has brought attention to us from several people seated at the table next to us.

They took notice of Nick; they stared and leaned towards each other whispering. We usually ignored this behavior as we were used to it by now. The server brought us our food and we dug in. I was eating pancakes and sharing it with Nick. The whole time, I felt as though someone was looking at us. I looked at the table next us. It seemed as though they had not had their fill of staring and it was really getting to me.

My husband and kids were munching, enjoying their food. I placed a bite in my mouth but could not swallow. My emotions were getting to me and my tears start dropping onto my food.

I was thinking about how we were just a regular family, eating out and I couldn't enjoy myself, because these people at the other table were relentless with their scrutiny. Michael looked at me and saw the tears; he gave me a small reassuring smile, then flagged the server down and asked for the check. He and the kids were not even finished with their meal.

CHAPTER EIGHT

Nicholas has captured the heart of a reporter who wrote for an extremely prominent newspaper. He was present for the many amazing milestones in Nick's life, starting at a few months old and until Nick turned 16.

Sharing so many wonderful moments in our life, he became a personal friend of our family. One of his front-page articles led a prosthetic and orthotic company owner to approach us, offering to create prosthetic legs for nine-month-old Nick.

This may seem like great news but I was quite leery. We had been to two other well-known children's medical facilities who told me they could not do anything until he was three. At one such facility, it was suggested to amputate his finger so a prosthetic hand could be placed on his arm. So **not** going to happen! The other facility suggested bone lengthening his—very small but present—thighbones once he is older. At this point, we decided it was best to hold off searching for adaptations, and simply allow Nick to grow and develop at his own pace.

After much consideration, we realized we should not let this opportunity pass him by. We scheduled an appointment with the company owner and brought Nick to his facility. With the creativity and determination of the owner and his assistant, they were able to develop a design for prosthetic legs. They used a sturdy plastic frame in which Nick's body could be placed and modular foam legs could be changed as he grew.

The men used artificial shoulder and elbow joints to simulate the ultra-flexible joints of a developing toddler. This would give Nick the ability to sit in a car seat or walker and develop a healthy upright seating posture. At our second visit, we were told to buy Nick pants and shoes. When these words finally registered in my brain, my head almost exploded! I was so ecstatic that we could buy him shoes! Size 3. I bought two of pairs of sneakers and little work boots—sooooo cute.

It took one month after Nicholas was measured to complete the legs. It was the first day of spring that my three other children, both sets of grandparents, and of course our endeared reporter had gathered in the living room. We were so excited, because it was the day Nick's legs would arrive.

We were given instructions on how to fasten the device using swivel joints that could be locked into position at the hips, knees, and ankles. The legs were covered with a flesh-colored stockinet material.

Since growth spurts are an issue with children, the legs were completely modular. As Nick grew, the device could be taken apart to replace his metal calves and thighs with longer lengths. The legs were attached to a shell made of polypropylene plastic with plenty of air holes and Velcro bands. We had to pay much attention to his spine so the device would not put pressure on his bones or cause any sore spots. An outer plastic shell with a soft inner sheath was made to provide cushioning and room to grow. I could not wait to dress them up!

CHAPTER NINE

Life is great with Nick's legs. I can change his pants and shoes—to us, this was huge. I gave Marisa and Mike a pair of Nick's shoes and told them to go outside and scuff up the bottoms. They totally got it, so out they went onto the driveway to dirty them up.

Meghan loves the legs too, when not attached to Nick she used them to practice tying shoelaces—nothing like multipurpose prosthetics. I could now place Nick in a shopping cart without the worry that he would fall out.

The kids and I pile into the car and headed to the store. On the way, I mentally prepare myself because people would stare—this is a very common occurrence when going out in public.

I pushed Nick in the cart up and down the food aisle while Marisa perused ahead of us, picking out all their favorite snacks. Mike and Meghan were in the clothing section, playing hide and seek amongst the clothes racks.

47

I noticed a woman stalking me, trying to get a closer view of Nick. More often than not, I usually just smiled at the staring people and give them an opening if they want to ask me questions.

After I completed most of my food shopping, the stalker lady continued to trail me. I finally turned around and gave her the look—what is your problem? Hesitantly, she asks what happened to him.

At this point, I had no patience left. It could be the inappropriate behavior of the hide-and-seek siblings, or the fact I hate food shopping, I'm not sure. Not being able to give my practiced answer of "he was born this way", I said a little too loudly, mixed with anger, "Miracle Grow and Baby Magic didn't work!"

The woman was shocked at my outburst and turned a few shades of red, I completely embarrassed her. I felt sooooo bad as she hurried away. I promised myself to work on my sense of humor.

CHAPTER TEN

If I had to describe myself, which I really do not like to do. I would say, overall, I am a kind and patient person, and quiet until I am comfortable with the people around me. My mother instilled in me to **always** behave like a lady, and my faith in Christ inspired me to be a good Christian, but lately I've become a total stranger – even to myself. I am more emotional than I have ever been, I cry too often and become frustrated easily. This simply is not me, and I need to do something about it.

I made an appointment to see my general practitioner; I trust her and knew I could tell her anything. I was seated in the exam room and had Nicholas in his car seat. It was too hot out to put his legs on without being soaked in perspiration. He was entertaining himself with his toys dangling from the handle.

My doctor entered the room and asked how I was doing, I opened my mouth to talk, and nothing resembling the

English language came out. I started sobbing as I tried to explain what was wrong; I couldn't, so I just point at Nick.

She bent down to look at him as he happily gave her his attention. She rubbed his little cheek and states that he was beautiful, and she understood. After I calmed down, she asked me a barrage of questions. She continued to explain that I was suffering from P.T.S.D.—Post Traumatic Stress Syndrome, a condition that results in a series of emotional and physical reactions in individuals who have either witnessed or experienced traumatic events. She said she was surprised I did not seek her help sooner and prescribed me medication. It was a huge relief that it was treatable.

CHAPTER ELEVEN

Nick adapted quickly to his new legs, but this one morning he sat in our family room, playing with the toys I placed between his legs; he fell backwards on the carpet. There he lay on his back with the legs sticking straight up in the air. I could not help it; I burst out laughing. I know that sounds mean but I never thought he would be in a position to fall down. He was not hurt, just taken by surprise.

I managed to keep Nicholas on track developmentally. This was extremely important to me and a goal I refused to back down from. He was so bright; he smiled, babbled, he could lift his head and chest, roll over and swat at dangling objects. He could even drink on his own from a sippy cup.

I read to him and he could point to objects in the book when prompted. He started to crawl. While on his belly, he would put his arm in front of him and wiggle each side of his butt forward. This is how he moved to wherever he wanted to go. If he did not like the direction he was facing, he would

51

push himself up with his arm and pivot to where he was aiming for. Then, off he went, heading for the door down the hall where Nana and Pop Pop live.

Bang-bang-bang on the door. He's, yelling, "Nana". She answered from the other side, "Who's banging on my door?"

Before it opens, belly laughs gave Nick away.

We have all gradually progressed into a routine with some days more relevant than others. My father-in-law was diagnosed with Stomach Cancer before Nick was born, but with surgery and chemo treatments he seemed to be on the road to recovery. A couple of months later, he had relapsed and began chemo again, which left him very weak.

So, in the evenings after dinner, I would bath and dress Nick and bring him over to my in-laws. My father-in-law loved this one particular family show, and would watch it every night. He knew that when it came on, it was Nick and Pop Pop time. Settling on the couch, my father-in-law propped his arm up on a pillow where I would place Nick, half on his arm and half on the pillow. I'd ask, "Are ya good?" He said, "Yeah, we're chilling".

When Nick was six months old, tragedy struck our family again; my father-in-law passed away. I was so deeply heartbroken because he and I were so very close; I am so very grateful he held on and had the opportunity to spend time with Nick.

CHAPTER TWELVE

Once a week, Nick went to Occupational and Physical therapy. The room had a preschool class setting where they promoted social, cognitive, language, and physical development through a variety of fun—but educational— therapeutic activities. Six other children participated. The kids are excited and happy to see each other. The therapist has them interacting in games and exercise. Snack time is—without a doubt— their favorite. OPT is truly an enjoyable time—not only for our children, but also for us Moms.

There is an indescribable camaraderie among the mothers. We give each other strength and support. When one of our children completes a task that has taken weeks to accomplish, we all celebrate as if it is our own child. It is here we can talk about our true feelings without fear of judgment.

Nick sat at a table with his friends; they were waiting patiently for their snacks. The therapists handed out finger foods to enhance fine motor skills. Since Nick could not pick up his snack, I always sat next to him and fed him as I watched the other children tackle this endeavor.

One day, I asked one of the therapists if she could adapt something so he could pick up food and other items too. She looked at Nick, shook her head no, and said there was not any type of gripping device he could use that would enable him to pick up anything. She proposed that maybe there would be something when he's much older. . . .

Driving home, I was both furious and frustrated; my goal is to keep Nick on track and **progressing** like a regular kid. I refused to tolerate or accept that he couldn't do something. I just had to figure out how to help him do so.

Once home, I rummaged through all our kitchen drawers, looking for anything that might enable me to make Nick a thumb. Then I saw it! In one of the drawers I found a kazoo that belonged to one of my other kids; it was the perfect length and width for Nick's finger and chubby palm. First, I wrapped the three-inch long kazoo with a couple of rubber bands to give it grip, and then I attached it to Nick's left wrist with a band of Velcro. He looked at me strangely, probably wondering why I attached something to his hand. I placed him in his highchair and told him that I was going to make him waffles. He rewarded me with a big smile, because he loved waffles.

I took his hand and told him to move his finger up and down against the kazoo. We practiced this for a few minutes, and then I placed the cut pieces of waffle in front of him and showed him with my own fingers how to pick them up.

Instinctively, he knew how to use the contraption as a pincer finger. A few tries later, he managed to put the waffle into his mouth. I started cheering loudly, "Yeah! You are such a big boy! Look at you feeding yourself".

My praise put a huge smile on Nick's face. As he continued to try to feed himself, I ran down the hall, yelling for my mother-in-law. She heard me calling her and opened her door to her house. I ran into her home, jumping for joy and full of smiles. I told her to hurry up and go in the kitchen.

As she rounded the corner, she saw what Nick was doing. Simultaneously, Nick saw his Nana and a huge smile emerged on his little face. Nick earned Nana's signature expression for all of her grandchildren who did a good job, "Yeah for Nick! Two thumbs up!"

Next, I called Michael to tell him to stop at home because I taught Nick how to feed himself. By the time he was able to stop at home, I had Nick picking up plastic play coins and dropping them in an empty coffee can. He was having a great time, laughing every time the coin made a clunking sound as it hit the bottom of the can. Michael looked at the contraption on Nick's left hand, raised his eyebrows and asked wearily, "What is that?" I told him it's mothering genius at work.

The next time we go to therapy, I bring the kazoo along. Nick and I showed the therapists what he could do; they are very surprised and thrilled. Nick could now participate in motor skills and snack time with finger foods. The occupational therapist asked me to bring a spoon from home next week. I had given her an idea to fashion a spoon that could be attached to his wrist.

CHAPTER THIRTEEN

Nicholas was eleven months old when we decided to buy him a wheelchair. This required that we travel to another county to meet with a certified rehabilitation specialist who was able to design a state-of-art wheelchair. It had all the bells and whistles that could carry Nick until adulthood.

The new wheels were customized with a joystick that Nick could push or pull. In addition, it had a remote control with a kill switch for us, just in case curiosity wills him to ignore his obedient side. The chair could accommodate his prosthetic legs, but he could also sit in the chair without them. At the push of a button, the seat lowered to the floor, enabling Nick to get in and out on his own. Another button would lift him to table height.

At this particular appointment, the primary goal was to take precise measurements of Nick to ensure the wheelchair was a specific fit.

The facility where the fitting took place was a rehabilitation center for those who have mental and/or physical disabilities. It catered to everyone from toddlers to young adults. Some patients were in wheelchairs while others used walkers or had braces on their legs. The facility offered residential services, but many people, only attended out-patient rehabilitation.

I looked affectionately at the children in the building. Most of them had a long road ahead of them, and once again I was reminded of how truly blessed we were that Nick was only missing limbs. Our child was a living testimony to the fact that we must never discount the work of God. Nick exposed the medical community's too-frequent claim to omniscience, and too rare allowance for God and his miracles or the power of the human spirit.

We are at the final visit to the rehabilitation center. Nick's bright red wheelchair is complete, and he now has the opportunity to take a test drive. He is the youngest person to operate a Permobil. Once he is placed in the seat and belted in the specialist instructs him how to operate the joystick that's attached on the left side of the arm rest, she teaches him the different directions he can go by either pushing or pulling the joystick making the chair go left or right, forward or backward. He catches on pretty quickly, and then off he goes—zooming down the hallway with us chasing after him.

When he reaches the end of the hallway, he turns the chair around with a huge smile plastered on his face. It is clear he's reveling in his newfound freedom. Now where's that remote with the kill switch?

CHAPTER FOURTEEN

It's Nick's first birthday, and there were at least four hundred people gathered throughout Pickell Park.

If you walked four miles around the park, you could enjoy the festivities and entertainment; you could even take photos with seven different food chain characters. Food and beverages were served from food trucks and the sugar rush was provided by a crowd favorite—a five-foot high ice-cream sundae and three full sheet birthday cakes.

The DJ provided the music and the gazebos were turned into dance floors. It's a walk-a-thon! The walk-a-thon was organized by a group of amazing women and men, and one kick-ass cousin who spent hundreds of hours arranging all the food and festivities.

The school year for my other children was drawing to an end; they only had one month left until summer break. My oldest, Marisa, was in eighth grade; she wrote a poem for a school project and had to bring in an object that was related to the poem. She told me she wrote a poem about her baby brother.

His smile brightens up my day, His little voice of laugh and play
He does things in his own special way, His happy spirit is here to
stay, and He is a small boy, this child meek and mild, baby of our
dreams, our very Special child.
By: Marisa Santonastasso

Of course, I brought him to her class! The kids and the teacher were very excited to meet Nick. They wanted to know if they could ask me questions, so for forty-five minutes, we had a very interesting question and answer session.

One of Marisa's classmates had such a deep question and I can remember it like it was yesterday.

"Do you have more appreciation and love for your other children since Nick was born?"

How profound for a young student.

I answered without hesitation, "No, I love and appreciate them equally now as I did before".

I thought a lot about what that child asked. In our family you never go out the door or hang up the phone without an "I love you". This is so important to Michael and me—and yes, even now, we still say I love you before we go out the door, hang up the phone or end a text.

CHAPTER FIFTEEN

It was time for Nick to visit the specialist, so I called the office to schedule an appointment. I spoke with the receptionist who gave me the date and time, and I wanted to inform the office of his condition so as to avoid any negative reactions they may accidently express. I did not want Nick to become upset if someone should have a negative reaction to him.

I said to her, "I just want to let your office know that Nick only has only one arm, so we can avoid the shock factor."

She replied, "That's okay, honey. We've seen children with an amputated arm before."

"No, you don't understand. He only has one arm," I explained and paused to take a breath, but she interjected before I could continue.

"Oh, okay. I understand now."

I'm thinking to myself, Lady you have no clue… Aloud, I say, "Wonderful…"

Just as I'm about to say more, she says, "I will put a note in his chart about his arm."

I begin again "He only has one arm that ends with a finger, and his other arm is a stump just below the shoulder.

She interrupts again, and says, "I will note that."

She's ready to end the call when I yell, "Wait! I'm trying to tell you he only has one arm and the right is a little stump, and he doesn't have any legs…"

Silent seconds go by, and I feel compelled to check in. "Hello? Are you still there?"

I heard a bang and perhaps shuffling of papers. I believe she may have dropped the phone.

I blew out a huffy breath, and said, "Helllooo?"

"Yes, Mrs. Santonastasso I'm still here. We will see you soon." She hung up.

I hoped not all doctor visits would be like this, because I rightly predicted that there would be many more in the future.

CHAPTER SIXTEEN

It was summer.

Nick was 14 months old when my family was invited to a softball tournament hosted by a local lodge. Each year the lodge would choose a local family as the beneficiary. Organizers of the annual memorial softball tournament hoped to raise $10,000 on Nick's behalf.

It was difficult—mentally and emotionally—to accept assistance. We never asked for handouts, but we needed to drop our pride to raise our child, so we appreciated everything that came our way.

There were twenty men's teams and four women's teams. Each team wore t-shirts advertising businesses or a child they were sponsoring. One women's team was named Nick's Girls.

Local businesses donated cash, food, and drinks that were sold at the games and each participating team paid an entry fee to compete. The umpires offered their services free of charge.

Thirty games were played on softball diamonds in two towns. After four teams have been declared champions, hundreds of players gathered at the lodge for a post-tournament celebration with food, drinks, entertainment, and a fundraising auction of sports memorabilia.

Each year, we were invited back to attend this annual charity event, and to offer our support to other families who face astronomical medical costs because of their children's health.

The members of the lodge and past recipients became extended family.

There are no words to truly express our deepest gratitude to these selfless people who took embracing families of children with disabilities to a higher level. Months of preparation and hundreds of man-hours are invested each year to make certain that the event is a success, and they are the most humble people I've ever met.

Their motto: **"It's all about the kids!"**

CHAPTER SEVENTEEN

Marisa used to eat, breathe, and sleep gymnastics. She constantly walked around the house in handstand mode. We had to be cautious because we never knew when her feet would be flying towards our faces.

One day, I walked into the TV room and found her teaching Nick how to do a handstand. His butt was straight in the air, while he leaned on his right shoulder and balancing his body using his left hand. He was so excited he could do a handstand like his sister.

This was a pivotal step towards his independence; he eventually used this technique to climb onto everything. That's how we came to find him one day, dancing on the kitchen table to music from the TV. Michael looked at me, smiled and said, "He's going to be okay."

He was speaking about Nick's future, but my immediate concern was teaching him how to get down. I got this! I put pillows on the floor next to the couch and placed

66

Nick on the couch on his belly. I told him to wiggle until his bottom hung off the couch. I held his waist and he slowly slid down the cushion until his bottom hit the pillows. Once he was down to the floor, he turned around with a big smile and he told me he wanted to do it again.

Michael was outside maintaining the landscape where the kids were playing; like all our neighbors, we had a huge backyard in a beautiful country living setting. A brook flowed through the middle our property, so Michael built a bridge to access the other side so that we could enjoy the basketball court and playground equipment. There was a wooden balance beam for Marisa and her friends to practice gymnastics, and a platform tree stand where my husband and my son, Mike, could practice shooting their bow and arrow for hunting.

My husband watched as Marisa, Mike, and Meghan ran towards the bridge in a race to see who would reach the other side first; Nick was speeding in his wheelchair, following in their footsteps to catch up with his siblings.

Marisa had just turned around to check on Nick as the front tires of his wheelchair hit the edge of the bridge, causing the chair to come to a sudden dead stop. The seatbelt had no power to stop Nick from flipping out of the seat head-over-bottom, and landing on his back with a thud.

He was too stunned to cry, having the air knocked out of him. The loud thud caused Mike and Meghan to turn in his direction, and they started yelling and crying. Michael ran and picked Nick up, checking for injuries. Marisa ran, shouting as she came through the kitchen door to tell me that Nick had an accident.

As I ran out the door heading toward the yard, Michael carried Nick towards the house. He was not crying, just shaken up. Nick reached for me as Michael put him in my arms. We all piled into the kitchen for a closer inspection while my husband explained to me what happened.

Marisa nodded in agreement, adding, "He did a perfect flip in the air! I would score it a ten."

Always the gymnast.

CHAPTER EIGHTEEN

Summer was drawing to an end and it was time for back-to-school shopping. I called out to the kids to get ready. Marisa shouted, "I'll get Nick".

Mike added, "I'll get Aliss."—It's the nickname for Nick's prosthetic legs—and when put together, Nick and Aliss sounds out Nicholas.

We were headed to the mall. I used a stroller for Nick, since the wheelchair weighs three-hundred pounds and does not fit in our vehicles.

We were in a children's clothing store. I pushed Nick through the aisles while Michael helped the kids pick out their sizes. Their arms were laden with clothes they needed to try on. The store was extremely crowded and we needed to wait for dressing rooms. Other parents and children gathered in the area, also waiting. The adults looked ready to rip their hair out, and the kids were antsy. The waiting continued as kids emerged from the dressing room only to grab another heap of clothing from their parents.

Bystanders started to look around and their eyes landed on Nick. I handed him a cookie, and he took the gooey deliciousness between his left finger and short right arm. He lifted it to his mouth and hummed, "Yummmm".

The stare-fest intensified, but not for long. Michael, the kids, and I have honed our skills of blocking Nick from unwelcome prying; we each stepped into place and created a circle with him in the middle.

CHAPTER NINETEEN

If I couldn't find Nick watching television or playing with his toys in the TV room, chances were pretty good he was at his Nana's house just down the hall. I walked into her living room to find Nick on the couch eating maple brown sugar oatmeal. Not twenty minutes ago, I asked him if he wanted oatmeal for breakfast, and he told me no.

He looked at me with a shit-eating grin on his face. In a huff, I say, "I just asked you if you wanted oatmeal and you told me no."

His answer, "You don't make it like Nana".

I am guessing it must be the fact that she stirs the instant oatmeal in the opposite direction then I do, since we buy the same brand.

My mother-in-law was also wearing a smile, but it was because she and Nick had a surprise.

They told me to stay on the couch as my mother-in-law took Nick into the kitchen. I wondered what they were up to. Finally, they said, "Okay, you can come in the kitchen now". Nick was **walking** towards me, balanced on his tiny thighs, and moving his hips individually in a swishing motion, taking super small "steps". I bent down low and opened my arms wide until he reached me.

My cheeks hurt from smiling so wide. My eyes were blurry from happy tears. I hugged him extra tight and swallowed hard until I choked out the words in his ear, "I'm so proud of you!"

He leaned back to look at my face, and we both smiled. My mother-in-law smiled happily as she explained to me how they had been practicing for a while and wanted to surprise me. I lifted Nick high in the air and said, "Let's call daddy!"

CHAPTER TWENTY

I was so excited!

Nick was old enough for preschool; I was employed at the preschool my other children attended, but this time I just wanted some free time for chores or running errands. I called a local Christian preschool to register Nick.

I spoke with the director of the program and began to explain Nick's situation. She replied that she was familiar with my family, and would need time to consider his registration. I thought this was strange and wondered why she would need time to consider.

She took down my phone number and told me she would call back. Later that afternoon, the director called back and informed me that it was not possible for Nick to attend. She felt that it would have been unfair to expect the staff to devote too much attention to one child, since he would need to be carried by a staff member during the two-and-a-half hour session, especially up and down stairs.

I could not believe what I was hearing. I told her that my child was not a monkey, and that he did not need to be hanging on the neck of a staff member the entire "two-and-a-half hour session". I wanted him to participate, just as the other children did. I did thank her "for nothing" when I hung up.

After a cursing shit storm, I called another preschool. I was determined to have Nick enrolled, even if I had to call every preschool in the county. I spoke with the director and once again explained Nick. Before she could say anything, I told her about the previous call and what had transpired. I also quickly added that Nick attended a similar program and was an independent and able child.

Without any hesitation, the director invited Nick and I to visit. The next morning when I dressed Nick, I explained that we were going to visit a new school where he would make new friends, learn, and play. A big smile appeared on his face—always the happy child.

The director and head teacher welcomed us warmly and led us to a large classroom. The little students were playing at different activity tables spread throughout the room. Nick sat on my lap at a table with the director and teacher, as we discussed the curriculum. Nick struggled with me to put him down; the director noticed and gave me permission to let him loose.

He immediately went to the carpeted area where different trucks were scattered around and two little boys were playing. Nick put his hand on top of a truck, moving it back and forth while making engine noises. The two boys joined Nick with their trucks, and the next thing, they had created a monster truck event, complete with loud crashing noises which quickly captured the attention of other children to their group.

The children easily accepted Nick, and I hoped the staff would react the same way.

The head teacher showed me her plan book and asked if I thought Nick would have any trouble participating in any of the scheduled activities. I looked over her plans and with a confident smile on my face, confirmed he would not have a problem. They returned the smile.

We continued the discussion, considering the possibility of having an aide available if Nick should need any assistance. The director offered to place the advertisement in the newspaper for a part-time aide; she would also be in charge of interviewing all prospects and afford me an opportunity to meet the aide and make the final decision. She explained that the aide will be considered a staff member, but she will not be on the school's payroll. I would have to pay her salary in my own capacity for her to be Nick's personal aide. About a week later, the director called me for a meeting with a potential aide; she had just retired as a school bus driver. Nick and I went to the school, where we met the most wonderful older woman.

After chatting for a while, she stated that she **had** to be Nick's aide; that God put it in her heart. Intuition told me there was no doubt; I could trust her with Nick.

"Now the big question," she started. "How and when do we help Nick?"

I answered "You don't. He will tell you if he needs help."

CHAPTER TWENTY-ONE

That weekend was very busy; Marisa had a gymnastics meet. She was running around the house, grabbing her gym bag and snacks.

Michael has taken Mike and Meghan out for the day. The only thing left for me to do was to get Nick ready.

I could hear the TV and Nick singing. The big, purple dinosaur was his absolute favorite, and he has at least twenty videos that play non-stop. He was laying on his side, moving his arm from his head to his shoulder then his belly and bottom.

I asked," What are you doing?" He was too into the TV to answer me, and continued to sing, "Head and shoulders, knees and toes".

I wanted to burst out laughing, because he was so damn cute, but I didn't. I was actually in awe of his self-perception. To our family, he wasn't challenged or disabled;

that was society's conclusion for people who don't fit the norm.

Marisa opened the kitchen door and spotted me having coffee at the breakfast bar; half of her body was in the kitchen and the other half outside, holding Nick. The kids have been playing on the swing-set that sat a couple of feet away from the deck attached to our house.

Nick has been able to get to the swing set and sandbox unassisted. I was wondering why she was holding him. "Don't get mad when you see Nick. We [meaning her, Mike, and Meg] were watching him."

Immediately, I thought he was hurt and cautiously asked, "Why do you think I would be mad?"

She stepped fully into the kitchen so I could see Nick. He was covered in dirt from head to bottom. His clothes were grass-stained and there was absolutely not one part of him that was not soiled.

Relieved he was not hurt, I started laughing. Marisa blew out the breath she's been holding, and shouted out the door to her two conspirators, "She's not mad!"

How could I be mad when they completely showed Nick no mercy? To them, he was just one of the gang. Now **they** had to bathe him.

CHAPTER TWENTY-TWO

Beep-beep-beep!

The alarm went off as Nick and I walked through the metal detector at the airport.

A security person waved the wand up and down Nick, and it's lit up like crazy. I wanted to laugh, but safety is a serious matter.

"It's the rods in his prosthetic legs," I say as the security guard looks at Nick and me suspiciously.

We are really holding up the line. Marisa, her best friend, and the girl's mother are waiting for us with Nick's stroller. It seemed as though my explanation was not sinking in, so I twisted Nick's foot backwards.

"See? Fake legs. That's why he's beeping."

The startled guard nodded and said, "GO".

Nick could be extremely heavy when he wore his prosthetic legs. After carrying him for a long time, my arms felt as though they were breaking. I was nervous and perspiring profusely when we boarded the plane.

Marisa took the end seat so she could talk to her friend across the aisle, while Nick sat on my lap in the middle seat. I hoped no one would take the window seat, but no such luck.

An older gentleman checked his ticket and looked right at me. "I'm the window seat," he stated.

I told Marisa to stand up so the gentleman could make his way into his seat. I stood and tried to turn Nick around so I could slide back into the aisle. Nick's body turned, but not his legs; they were caught on the armrest. From the man's expression, he was obviously not thrilled at the thought of having to sit next to us. He was probably praying that Nick would not start crying.

He should have been more worried about me crying; my nerves were fried and his judgmental appearance did not help matters.

Finally, we managed to free the legs of the armrest, and the man was able to sit in his seat. Nick slept for the entire duration of the flight.

We arrived in Orlando Florida without any further incident.

Marisa and her gymnastics team were competing in a very important competition. After the two-day event, we had time to visit a theme park. The girls were very excited, exploring every square inch. The parents tried to keep up with the young athletes, which was comical.

We walked for hours, sweating our asses off until we finally let them go off on their own with all the warnings—stay together, don't go to the bathroom alone, watch the time, don't be stolen, and let's meet up for lunch.

The girls decided on a restaurant where they wanted to eat. As we entered, Nick's eyes grew wide, as he took in the scene; there were different themed dining areas, and we were seated in a jungle.

Nick sat in a booster seat—completely taken with his surrounds. It was really loud in our dining area; the girls were talking and there were jungle noises.

Our food arrived and everything looked delicious—I was starving! Nick had his plate of chicken nuggets and fries, and I ordered a cheeseburger.

Just as I was about to take a bite, the room went dark, thunder boomed loudly, lightning flashed, and the sound of rain pouring down filled the room.

I looked at Nick; he had the biggest boo-boo lip and tears filled his eyes. It broke my heart. I stood and grabbed him quickly out of the booster seat. He hugged me—his arm tight around my neck—and looked over my shoulder. **And then,** right behind me, a gigantic gorilla came flying out from the tree cover, beating its chest rapidly and roaring. I didn't

81

know who was louder—the gorilla, or Nick screaming at the top of his lungs, traumatized for life.

I did not think we would be dining in this restaurant in the future.

CHAPTER TWENTY-THREE

It was déjà vu when I received a call from Meghan's first grade teacher.

She asked if I would come to the classroom when I picked Meghan up from school. My mother-in-law offered to watch Nick, so I could meet with the teacher. As I walked into the classroom, I saw Meghan at her desk; she looked up unconcerned, and I was relieved she didn't appear to be upset.

The teacher greeted me and indicated that I should take a seat. She then placed Meg's drawing on the table and explained that the students were instructed to draw a picture of their family.

I looked at the drawing and saw what she's drawn. Her dad, me, Marisa, Mike, Nick, and herself—I thought she did a really great job…

I looked at the teacher who appeared disturbingly perplexed, and asked, "Do you see the problem here?" She pointed to Nick.

I looked at the picture again and shook my head. I could not see the problem.

Concern clouded her face as she explained, "Meghan drew everyone anatomically correct except her brother, and I'm curious whether there are issues".

I looked once again, and saw that Meg drew Nick without legs and his one arm. I speculated that the teacher might have been new to the school system and therefore, may not be familiar with our family as the other staff members have become since Marisa and Mike have attended this small school.

I stood up, explaining that Nick was born that way. I explained that his siblings adore and care for him very much, and I was certain there were no issues. I motioned for Meg to come to me. When she did, I grabbed her little hand in mine and started walking towards the door; I looked back at the teacher with a smile and said "I'm expecting her to receive a good grade, since she draws so anatomically correct".

I couldn't wait for Meg to bring the picture home so it could go on the refrigerator; but I feared for the child who drew stick figures. Would their parents receive a call, too?

CHAPTER TWENTY-FOUR

"Who's ready for a big boy bed?" I asked Nick. He looked at me with a funny face waiting for me to elaborate. I told him to go upstairs to Mike's room, which took him completely by surprise.

He climbed the stairs by placing his left arm on the stair and lifting his body up onto the step. He did this repeatedly and quickly until he reached the top landing. His brother's room is a few more feet down the hall.

Nick looks into the room where there are now two single beds; one has mesh safety rails on each side and is decorated with camouflage bedding. I picked him up and placed him in the middle, and said, "Try it out".

He threw himself face-first into the pillow, and then rolled onto his back. He had a huge smile on his face.

I asked, "Do you love it?"

He shook his head and yelled, "Yessss!"

I explained to him that he would be sharing this room with Mike, and that he would be sleeping here. He sat up to take in his new room all decked out in a hunting theme.

Mike was more than happy to share his room with Nick and told me he would take care of his little brother—even if he woke up in the middle of the night. Oh, and he would turn on the bathroom light if needed.

CHAPTER TWENTY-FIVE

We were warned that couples sometimes divorce or separate when facing a crisis involving a severe detriment to their child. Sometimes, couples cannot handle a life altering situation while managing the intricacies of marriage.

That is not **us**. We are considered a "power couple".

Michael is one of the strongest people I know; he always has his "shit" together—even after the birth of Nick and six months later, the passing of his father. He is a pillar of strength for me, his children, his mother, five sisters, and brother.

It came as a huge shock to receive a call from a gentleman from my husband's office, telling me Michael has been taken to the hospital. Of course, I went into a panic, asking what happened, but he wouldn't explain. He just told me to head over to the hospital.

I ran Nick over to my mother-in-law's home and told her about the call. She met me at the hospital after my friend showed up to watch Nick.

I arrived at the hospital to find Michael in the emergency room. He was transported by ambulance. My panic lessened when I saw him lying on the bed, awake but extremely pale. He was hooked up to various machines.

I reached over the bed railing to give him a kiss, hold his hand and ask what happened.

He said, "I woke up this morning like normal and went to my office. I sat at my desk when all the emotions of the last two years went through my mind. In less than a minute, I lost track of everything around me. I walked out of my office and was in the hall walking towards the center office. I slid down the wall, my heart started to race, my vision blurred, and I felt really weak".

Tears started raining down his face, and in a ragged breath, he continued to tell me, "I know I had to make it to a coworker's door to tell them to call 911; that I was having a heart attack. I told him not to call you because you have enough to deal with. I didn't think I was going to make the end of the day".

We were both sobbing. After a few minutes, we somewhat composed ourselves. I ask what happened to him after he hit the floor, and he said "The police showed up first and put me on oxygen. Then the paramedics showed up and started asking me questions. I told them I was having a heart attack. They put on the blood pressure cuff, opened my shirt, and hooked me up to the EKG. Then they put me on the stretcher and brought me here".

After blood work and some tests, the doctor came in to examine Michael. He asked multiple questions and said that he would be back later with the test results.

A nurse gave Michael medication to calm his nerves. My mother-in-law arrived and we updated her on what had happened. Michael was exhausted and slept for a little while.

Eventually, the doctor came in and informed him that he did not have a heart attack. His blood work and vital signs were good, and he may have experienced Tachycardia—a fast heart rate that is not caused by an underlying disease, but from exercise, fear, anxiety, stress, or anger.

There was no need for him to stay overnight and we were sent home. Still feeling exhausted, Michael stayed on the couch until dinner, went to bed early, and went back to work the next day.

He started experiencing the same symptoms in the afternoon, and immediately left his office. He drove to his doctor's office a mile away.

He walked in the front door feeling as though he was going to faint. He told receptionist that he felt as though he was having a heart attack and she immediately brought him into the exam room and started an EKG.

As the doctor was reading the results, she started to ask questions; the first one, "Aren't you Nick's dad?" Michael replied affirmatively.

After the Q&A, she told him everything appeared fine with his heart. She diagnosed him with anxiety attacks, which is common for people who hold in their emotions. The doctor prescribed a medication for anxiety and asked him to see her on a weekly basis for a couple of months.

Michael wanted everything perfect for everyone, especially seeing how certain things have affected the people in his family—whether it was the calls from schools, or other parents' attitudes. He continued pretending everything was okay, knowing that the right thing to do as a parent was to keep everybody safe and happy. He did not realize that by trying to maintain that façade, he was neglecting his own emotions.

CHAPTER TWENTY-SIX

It was a very hot summer day, and Marisa, Mike, Megan, and their friends were swimming in the above-ground pool. Nick was in his kiddy blow-up pool on the deck; he was totally happy and occupied, playing with pool toys and watching his sibling's shenanigans.

He was not a fan of the big pool. When any of us took him in, he would wrap his arm around your neck in a death grip. After buying different types of tubes and floats, we finally found a pink flamingo float in which he could sit and wrap his arm around the neck, which relieved his fear of falling in.

I was seated at the patio table, enjoying our recently-renovated deck that ran the full length of our house. The wood had been replaced with track decking that Michael and I installed ourselves—yup, we are weekend warriors.

Nick could walk out of our kitchen door, across the deck, and right to my mother-in-law's kitchen door. A couple of weeks ago the wood gave him multiple splinters in his hand, and his shorts would snag and rip. It seemed we solved the splinter problem but did not realize the plastic would become scalding hot from the sun and burn his hand. We had to have a custom awning installed, which completely shades the entire deck. It's a stay-cation for us.

CHAPTER TWENTY-SEVEN

Nick started Pre-K at the same pre-school he attended last year. He's very excited to see the familiar faces of his classmates. We were also blessed to have Nick's aide again as the two of them have grown very close; she told me often how much she loved Nicky.

In the past few months, he has progressed exceedingly well and has made many friends. His classmates are naturally aware to not step on him or knock him over, and they are eager to carry things for him. At circle time, they always have a space waiting for him. They accept him without prejudice— he's just one of the gang.

During fall, the children were excited for their field trip to the local pumpkin farm. I sat with Nick on the school bus as his chaperone—there was no way I would miss his first class trip.

The class went on a hayride pulled by a tractor, and then they went through the child-friendly haunted house. They picked their own pumpkins, after which they enjoyed apple cider and cookies. Nick told me his favorite part of the field trip was the ride on the school bus and he could not wait to tell his brother and sisters.

One afternoon, when I picked Nick up from school, a mother whose little boy was in Nick's class said she would like to have Nick over to play, since the boys have developed a close friendship. He was excited to go. We set up a time for the boys to get together.

When I dropped him off, the mom asked me if there was anything special she needed to do for Nick. Her son answered for me, telling his mom, "He doesn't need help and if he does, he'll tell me".

Okay, the boys have it all under control! It was his first play date without me; I was sick to my stomach and could not wait to pick him up. I needlessly worried; the boys had a great time and got together frequently.

CHAPTER TWENTY-EIGHT

It was Christmas break from school for all the kids, and my house resembled Grand Central Station. Marisa and Mike had friends over and Meghan was at the neighbor's house, shucking the horse stalls in exchange for riding lessons. A horse was at the very top of her Christmas wish list.

Christmas shopping was a nightmare; we bought bikes for Marisa and Mike, power wheels for Meghan—because no way is she getting a real horse—and the items on their Christmas wish lists.

Now, to find gifts for Nick. It was heart-wrenching going up and down the aisles trying to find the absolute right toys. We don't want him to feel cheated as the older kids received big ticket items. We settled for a football, a golf set, T-ball and bat, clothes, and a big plastic rocking horse. Most importantly, we bought more videos with the purple dinosaur. I felt like the Grinch has stolen Christmas.

My doorbell rang to announce a surprise visit from Nick's aide and her husband, who bought him a Christmas gift. We were all seated at the kitchen table, having coffee while Nick opened his gift; it is his very first action figure and he was so thrilled. After thanking them, he took his toy to the TV room to play.

I also thanked them very much for thinking of him. She looked at me with misty eyes and I knew immediately that something was wrong. She said she had to have a medical procedure, but the doctor assured her she could still be Nicky's aide. I allayed her fear and told her I wouldn't want it any other way. She sighed with relief and reminded me again that God put it in her heart to be a part of Nicky's life. Wow! That gave me goose bumps!

It was Christmas! I set the dining room table; I counted and recounted the table settings, making sure there are twenty-nine for our immediate family—fifteen adults and fourteen children produce the most incredibly wonderful chaos.

As I looked around the table, my heart filled with happiness. Michael woke me up at four in the morning just to open the oven door so he could shove the turkey in. Marisa woke up the siblings at five AM, shouting ""Santa was here!" We had hardly any sleep!" after we went to bed at two in the morning—waiting for the kids to actually fall asleep, and not pretend, so we could place the gifts under the tree.

Even after preparing and cooking food for hours, only for the meal to be over in less than forty five minutes, I was so grateful to be part of such a loving family who supported us through thick and thin.

A few more days and the kids would be back to school. I was more than ready, because they have turned the house into an obstacle course. They started by sitting on Nick's rocking horse and sliding it down the main staircase. Then they jumped into Meg's power wheels and raced towards the kitchen, jumped the threshold into the TV room, exited the vehicle, jumped on the couch over the side table to the love seat, screaming, "Don't touch the floor or you will be in the pits of under".

They ran up the kitchen stairs, through the hall, towards the main stairs where Mike's mattress sat at the top of the stairs. The four kids jumped on and wiggled it back and forth to slalom down the steps. They were headed straight for the front door which, thankfully, was closed, or they'd spill onto the road. My nerves were fried and I'd had enough! I was terrified that Nick would get hurt, but I knew it would not be right to stop him from participating. I firmly suggested they **all** watch a movie and bribed them with popcorn.

CHAPTER TWENTY-NINE

It was a Sunday morning in spring when I received a call from Nick's aide's husband. He said she had not been feeling well and made him promise to call me if anything happened to her.

He started crying while telling me she had passed away. I started sobbing when I heard this devastating news. He told me how much she loved Nick and how very happy she was to be part of his life.

I now had to explain to Nick that his aide would no longer be with him at school and that she had gone to heaven. Nick didn't say anything; he just cried. I asked him if he wanted to talk about it, and he answered, "No. I knew she loved me because she told me that all the time".

Nick just turned five and I brought cupcakes to his class, I spotted him enthusiastically clapping his arms together and singing with his classmates. He quickly walked—in his own special way—to a bin that was tall as he was, hooked his stunted right arm over the edge, scooped a sizable U-shaped block with his other arm, and tucked it under his chin.

In a flash, he was over at the construction site, had the block in place, and headed back for another.

Next, it was number time. Nick went to a seat at the table where his classmates were preparing to paint and glue their favorite number to sheets of construction paper. He painted the number ten pink and yellow by holding the paint bottle between his jaw and his right arm. Being right handed, he was extremely neat and stayed in the lines.

The light in the classroom flickered as the teacher says, "What time is it boys and girls?"

Nick and the other children sing, "Clean up. Clean up. Everybody clean up". Nick was right in the thick of things and swept a pile of Legos into a plastic bin. He did his share and his classmates seemed oblivious to his differences. With cleanup completed, the children gathered in a circle to talk about plans for graduation day.

There would be a play and Nick had two roles—as a camel and a horse. He nodded when the teacher asked him if he'd be able to do both. On Graduation Day, Nick marched down the aisle to Pomp and Circumstance with 21 other preschool graduates. He saluted the flag, sang songs, and enjoyed cookies and punch.

The director spoke to Michael and me while the children said their goodbyes. She told us that Nick's attendance in school has increased awareness and led the school to consider expanding with a new building that will accommodate physically challenged youngsters. She said that he had been a blessing, and that because of Nick, she had seen a tremendous growth on the part of the kids, parents, and staff interacting with someone "special".

CHAPTER THIRTY

We were steadily moving forward and ready for a new challenge. The only adaptive equipment Nick used was a spoon. All the special equipment served an important part in Nick's development, and he was ready for, his own power to take him where he needed to go. He was aware of his differences, but not verbal about it.

I explained this to the child study team when I registered Nick for Kindergarten, and for safety reasons, they insisted that Nick use his wheelchair. I countered that I did not want him sitting in a wheelchair during class and offered to purchase a seat with sides for his own personal use; they agreed to allow this if Nick could transfer himself from the wheelchair to the seat. I was able to research and purchase a Rifton chair. The company provided adaptive seating to meet the needs of clients of all ages and diagnoses with hi/lo or standard base options and positioning accessories. Nick's aide would only have to align the wheelchair next to his school chair and he would hop in; the wheelchair would remain in class and used for transporting only.

It was Nick's first day of Kindergarten and he was thrilled to take a bus to school. I brought him out to the bus in his wheelchair and onto the ramp that lifts him up into the bus. The driver locked his chair down with straps and started backing down the driveway. Nick waved goodbye with a huge smile on his face and I blew him some kisses. I have definitely always been one of those mothers who wanted to jump in my car to follow the bus to the school; but I did not—I'm headed to a coffee clutch.

Later that evening, my four children, Michael and I were eating dinner. The kids were talking all at once about their first day at school. I jokingly asked, "Who has homework?" and they all answered in unison, "I do".

NO, NO, NO—I hate homework! I didn't understand half the—shi—stuff they taught these kids. The curriculum is entirely different from when I went to school. Oh, let's not forget the school projects. They would forget to tell me about it until eleven the night before the project was due, and then there'd be a mad rush.

CHAPTER THIRTY-ONE

Life continued and ours was not entirely different from any other normal family. I stopped working to be a stay at home mom and to babysit for local families. In the evenings and weekends I was the designated mom taxi.

Marisa competed with her high school gymnastics team and club team. Mike wrestled with Mat Rats, and when time permitted, he hunted with Michael. Meghan was on the cheerleading team and loved horseback riding lessons at the neighbor's house. Most of my time was spent driving the kids back and forth. Nick was a great co-pilot and a big supporter of his siblings when we attended meets and matches. Parents of my children's teammates have become attached to Nick; they saved us seats on the bleachers so he could have the best view and some of the moms even brought him extra snacks.

Time swiftly went by and the holidays were approaching. Michael and I decided to take the kids and my mother-in-law on a vacation for Christmas.

It was late evening when we all piled in the SUV, which was loaded with luggage. As we pulled out of the driveway, I said, "Stop! I forgot something in the house." Michael pretended to be annoyed as him and I stepped out of the car and headed back into the house. We quickly gathered all the hidden presents and put them under the Christmas tree. We had assured our kids Santa would come to our house while we were away.

They were only receiving small gifts, because we just wanted to be together. Experiencing a magical theme park on Christmas Day is equal and most importantly to ensure one child wouldn't be getting more than the other would.

The theme parks were decorated in absolutely amazing holiday splendor. Michael was Nick's designated wheelchair driver, because it's really not easy to push a wheelchair through large crowds; you have to be cautious not to hit someone from behind, especially when they stop short in front of you. You also have to avoid somebody tripping and falling onto Nick.

Children darted in front of us, excited to see all the attractions, and unintentionally failed to pay attention. We had to be careful not to run them over. To get on rides, we parked

Nick's wheelchair with the strollers and Michael carried Nick as we waited in line—and let us not forget the stare fest.

After trying to board several rides and being told Nick was not tall enough, Michael and I were extremely annoyed. We did not want to cause a scene nor have our children see how deeply upset we were, so we continually explained that Nick would be on our lap or seated in between us as we held onto him. We were told it is against park policy—a liability—to allow him on a ride when he does not meet the safety requirements.

A park representative approached us and explained that if we used the wheelchair, Nick would be able to enjoy all the rides using the handicapped accessible entrances. This was a difficult decision we had to make; to us, the wheelchair is simply a mode of transportation—not a tool to get ahead on a line. We reluctantly took the handicapped option; it was more important for us to get Nick on the rides, because his sisters and brother refused to go on them without him.

CHAPTER THIRTY-TWO

We're anchored and the waves are rocking the boat up and down, "Get the net, get the net" Nick shouted as he slowly pulled up his crab line, Mike leaned over the side with the net and scoops up the crab, Nick anxiously waits for Mike to inspect his capture.

"It's a keeper!" Mike told Nick, and we all shouted, "Yeah!"

It was Nick's first crab that hadn't fallen off the line.

He usually pulled the line up too quickly, but he finally had it down to a science. He wrapped the line around his left finger, pulled up slowly, and then tucked the slacked line in between his chin and right arm. He repeated the process until the crab was close to the surface. His unwavering patience has paid off.

Marisa and Meg were on the other side of the boat, pulling up their crab lines—boys against girls. Everything seemed to be a friendly competition and Nick is shown no mercy, ever.

With the cooler full of blue claw crabs, we headed back to our house and docked the boat.

While Michael and Mike scrubbed down the boat, the girls and I set up the crab pot to cook the crabs; the smell of Old Bay permeated the house. Newspapers lined the patio table where the cooked crabs were customarily dumped in the middle. Hotdogs and hamburgers were cooked on the grill, and the mouthwatering aromas had us jumping into our seats—the time spent out on the water worked up our appetites.

Shouts came from the front of the house as several of the neighborhood kids made their way to our backyard; they were happy to see my children had come down for the weekend.

Mike and Meg jumped on their bikes with their friends to take a ride to the beach just around the corner while Marisa walked a couple of blocks to her friend's house. Nick walked across the backyard to play video games with his friend next door.

Michael and I enjoyed coffee in the sunroom and realized that our children did not have to be driven to their friend's houses anymore. The kids were able to have a game of basketball on the street, and they could ride their bikes in

107

the cul de sac where our shore house was located. This reminded us how we each grew up.

I lived in a large apartment complex and Michael grew up in a suburban neighborhood. We reminisced about how great it was that you only had to step outside to hang out with your friends, and you didn't have to come home until it was dark or your parents shouted for you. As much as we loved living in the country, we decided it would be great for our children to also have this experience. To my children's utter horror, we made the decision to move to the Jersey Shore permanently.

CHAPTER THIRTY-THREE

I tried to find Nick in the dark water of the lagoon. He fell off the dock and went under! I jumped in and kept diving down to find him, but I couldn't. I grabbed muck from the bottom. I came up to suck in a breath and dove down again. I still couldn't see anything. It was so dark, but I kept reaching around, hoping to get a hold of him. My heart was pounding out of my chest. My mind was screaming that he was going to drown.

Then I wake up—it's a nightmare, I'm gasping for breath, still panicked, and shake Michael awake. I tell him we can't move and recite my dream.

Our country home is already sold, but there is no way I am living on the water now. We have seen over a dozen homes with a realtor, finally we found a beautiful brand new tree-lined development. The neighborhood is filled with children of all ages who play outside on the front lawn and non-traffic road.

This was exactly what I wanted; we have a huge yard that backs up to a forest preserve. We are scheduled to move in April during Easter break. I believe Meghan is still traumatized because we moved on her birthday.

Marisa was in her senior year of high school, so we offered her the opportunity to live with her best friend until June or she could graduate early since she had enough credits. Marisa chose to move with us and would walk with her class at graduation in June to receive her diploma. Mike was registered for Middle school and Meghan and Nick were registered at the elementary school.

My kids were slowly adapting to their new surroundings, it was strange to them having neighboring homes closely sitting next to ours where our backyards shared a fence on the property lines.

After the first week of staying in the house, I suggested they go outside and make new friends; reluctantly Mike and Meghan decided to ride their bikes around the neighborhood and did meet many kids their age.

Nick would not leave the front of the house; he would skateboard up and down the driveway or stay on the sidewalk. I was really concerned by this behavior. He was always very outgoing and always a happy child. I wondered whether the move is a mistake, especially since his siblings also noticed he was not his usual self.

Meghan suggested they go outside and promised to keep him company, so Nick climbed onto his skateboard and tried spinning in a circle. The driveway had an incline and he's headed backwards toward the street, jumping off at the last second, laughing.

The kids across street, who are playing on their front yard, take notice. A boy about Nick's age and his older sister were watching, and Meghan called out, "Do you want to come over?" Without hesitation, the two kids run over. Thank God! Instant friendship!!!

CHAPTER THIRTY-FOUR

Michael, Nick, and I attended a meeting with the school principal and Nick's new second grade teacher. We were all seated in the office discussing Nick's curriculum from his previous school, and I could feel the immediate acceptance by their warm and astonished smiles. They were amazed by his accomplishments. Based on the research I did about this school system and the mission statement—which stated they would provide every student with a safe, supportive, **inclusive** and collaborative learning environment—I was confident we made a great decision to move to this town.

The teacher and Nick were engrossed in conversation, getting to know one another. She genuinely was in awe and radiated an excited intention for a smooth and happy transition to his new class. After establishing that he was able to keep up with his peers, she jovially asked if there was anything he couldn't do. I answered with a laugh, saying that

112

he couldn't swim; that he sinks right to the bottom. No worries, we're going to work on that.

Another school year was ending and we traveled to our previous town for Marisa's graduation from High School. Our family was so proud as we watched her receive her diploma. The graduating class is going on a trip for a celebration weekend. Before she left, I told her I needed a picture of her in the hallway that is named the "wall of fame", she rolls her eyes at me but does grant my request. "Smile please," I asked. She stood next to a photo plaque of herself for gymnastics. Yeah! One graduated, and three to go.

CHAPTER THIRTY-FIVE

I looked out the kitchen window and saw the now-finished in ground pool. The water sparkled as a brilliant shade of blue beckoned us to enter, promising relief from the stifling ninety-degree weather. Nick is on the steps practicing holding his breath underwater, this is the starting point for him to learn to swim, "How long was that" he asked as his head popped up from the water, "almost sixty seconds" I answered, he's been at this for close to two hours. I suggested we take a break for lunch and feared the goggles he wore would leave a permanent indentation across his forehead and around his eyes. A huge smile graced his sun-kissed face as he hopped up the stairs out of the pool and did a handstand onto the patio chair, saying, "I'm starving, but after I eat I'm practicing some more". I thought to myself of course you will, that's what Nick does, practices until he accomplishes his goals. *(You can watch a video on Nick's YouTube page to see how he swims.)*

Nick was in third grade when I received a call from the band teacher at his school telling me he would like to teach Nick to play the drums. He explained that they had an electric drum set he could play by attaching a drum stick to his left hand and a longer drum stick to his right arm.

Michael and I were totally thrilled about this opportunity for Nick—more than just the idea of Nick playing drums, but the fact his teachers didn't put limitations on him. I met with the band teacher after purchasing a sports tape that is sticky on both sides and would easily keep the drum sticks in place without cutting off his circulation.

It seemed as though Nick was gifted with an ear for music, which prompted us to buy him the exact set of electric drums to practice at home. At the music store, Michael looked at each type of drum pedals, and figured out that by reversing the hammer in the pedal Nick could sit on the pedals and with a slight jump with each of his thighs, would imitate stepping on them. Nick's perseverance paid off; and with the exceptional teaching of his band teacher, he became a member of the fifth grade band while still in third grade.

We just watched him play the drums at the winter music concert at his school. The final notes of his solo still lingered in the air as the applause for the band filled the auditorium. We all jumped to our feet and gave a standing ovation. Tears filled my eyes. I was in awe, and so proud of my kid.

115

Nick looked out across the crowd with a huge smile on his face. As his eyes landed on us, he gave us a chin up. He knew he crushed it.

CHAPTER THIRTY SIX

Thanks to the coordinated efforts of Marisa, Mike, and Meghan, I was able to return to work full time. They would make sure someone was home for Nick after school. I wished it was always that easy to assign chores.

Nick was not exempt. He was responsible for keeping his room clean, his clothes folded and put away, and most importantly, keeping our two little Yorkies fed. He was also responsible for taking them outside.

Michael attached door handles at Nick's height— to give him access to exit or enter the house— and he also had the garage door pad installed lower so Nick could reach it. We placed Nick's drinks and food on the lower shelves of the refrigerator and pantry and installed a second microwave on a credenza which he could reach to heat up his meals.

We made no fancy adaptions to our home. As Nick grew taller, he was able to reach almost everything. To make up his lack of height, he would use a kitchen chair.

We explained to him from a young age that the world would not adapt to him, but that he had to adapt to the world. "You need to do things Nick's way," is what we taught him. Our goal was to make him completely independent, because one day, we won't be here.

CHAPTER THIRTY-SEVEN

Every year, there's an abilities show in Edison. During our second year of attending, we were browsing each booth when we came across a vendor who had several hand cycles on display. Nick's eyes instantly lit up; he has spied a bright green bike he wanted to try.

The vendor gladly allowed Nick to try out the bike. Although it was a two-handle bike, Nick was able to pedal it using his left hand and steer using his right arm. We could tell he really wanted it.

The vendor and his wife introduced themselves to us. They offered us information about the variety of bikes and wheelchairs they carried and explained the advantages of having a wheelchair custom made for each user. He also used a wheelchair and gave us his invaluable perspective in this regard. He provided a heartfelt interpretation of how a person who needs to use a wheelchair feels.

We had Nick measured for a new wheelchair, and they offered to assist me with filing in the insurance forms. They said we could take the bike when the exhibit ended, so Nick would not have to wait the few weeks it would take if we placed the order. After buying a wheelchair and bike from them, I knew, without a doubt, that we would have many more transactions with this genuinely caring company.

Michael and Nick came through the front door, decked out in camo. Nick had a huge smile spread across his face, which answered my unspoken question.

They had gone to the Fish and Wildlife Center where Nick took the written exam for the hunter's safety course and a field test for his hunting license. He studied very hard and practiced many hours shooting my twenty-gauge shotgun.

Our favorite wheelchair company then helped us build an all-terrain camouflage hunting wheelchair which Michael attached a swivel gun-rest so Nick could shoot unaided. I gave Nick a super-tight, long hug. I was so proud of him, because I knew how long he has waited to go on hunting trips with his dad and brother and to enjoy the camaraderie of fellow hunters.

Through local news stories by our favorite reporter—and a serendipitous meeting with a wonderful woman—Nick was invited to several hunt clubs in New Jersey, Mississippi, and Kansas. The white tail mounts on our wall are testimony to his patience and diligence.

CHAPTER THIRTY-EIGHT

Meghan was on the driveway recording a video on her phone as Nick practiced tricks on his skateboard. They posted the video on YouTube, and in the first month, Nick had over 15,000 views.

Skateboarding is one of his favorite hobbies; he says it's freeing and when he goes fast, it feels as though he can fly.

Michael took him to the local skate park, where groups of teenagers were hanging out boarding, and was just about to suggest they leave and come back another time when one of the boys yelled out to Nick to join them. Nick did not think twice and headed towards the ramp to take his turn. He went down the half-pike, did a full turn and then tipped the front of his board up in the air to stop. The teenagers shouted out praises and encouraged him to do it again.

I never thought I would hear my happy, patient, sweet child scream his head off, throw a fit, and loose his patience until we bought him Gears of War for Xbox. Between the lag on the computer, the router going offline, and whatever else could go wrong, Nick went berserk.

He has on his Turtle Beach headset and did not realize how loud he was yelling. One of his best friends, who lived two doors down from us, often came over with his own controller and headset. They prepared to go into battle—both boys took the game very seriously and have invested hundreds of hours playing.

I was not thrilled about how much time they spent in front of the TV, but it afforded Nick the opportunity to participate and compete with other gamers who were unaware of the fact that he may have had a disadvantage. This has paid off; Nick was ranked in the top five—great job, "Chin for the Win".

Nick came in through the front door—his body was covered in sweat, his clothes were covered with dirt and grass stains, and the front of his shorts had huge rips in them – that was the third pair this week.

He knew I didn't care about the clothes as long as he was having fun doing the things he loved. His two friends came into the house through our garage, looking just as filthy as Nick. They walked past me towards the kitchen, and they all smelled of teenage spirit, swamp, and sweat.

I asked them where they'd been and Nick said they were at the lake, fishing, but it became too hot and they came home to swim. Two summers of practicing behind him, Nick could now jump off the diving board and swim the entire length of the pool.

I grabbed towels and put snacks and drinks on the patio table and asked Nick where his fishing pole was; he said the poles were put away in the garage. Good answer! He knew we didn't care about ripped or ruined clothing, but all the kids were responsible for their sports equipment.

However, it was time to order at least a dozen or more shorts for Nick. He wore a cargo style with an elastic waist that had allowed him to dress himself from a very young age. Thank God, I found a company where I could order shorts throughout the year.

I stood at the side pool and watched bubbles rise to the surface. Michael, Nick, and the scuba diving instructor were at the bottom of the pool. After a few hand signals, Nick starts swimming towards the other end of the pool with Michael following.

In another area of the pool, instructors were teaching a specialized class to people with challenges. The group of instructors are seriously dedicated to improving the physical and social wellbeing of people with disabilities through the sport of scuba diving. With the highest quality training, gentleness, and patience, the instructors' main goal was to help each class member earn their certification while accommodating each student's limitations.

Nick made his way back to the starting point unaided, but needed help rising to the surface due to the weights in the vest he was wearing. He spat out the mouthpiece, pushed off the facemask, wiped the water from his face and said, "That was awesome!"

Yes, it was.

CHAPTER THIRTY-NINE

In April, Nick's principal was notified that Nick had been selected as a statewide winner in the calendar poster contest sponsored by the NJ Task Force on Child Abuse and Neglect and the NJ State Parent and Teacher Association.

The contest asked students to design a poster about what makes a family strong. The poster Nick drew depicted a sturdy tree with roots that spelled out the word "love" and the sentiment "What makes a Family Strong is Deep-rooted Love". The poster will be published in the organization's 2009 calendar which was distributed in December.

On May twentieth—Nick's birthday—our family, his teacher, his principal and the school superintendent traveled to the Governor's mansion for an awards ceremony and lunch. A beautiful article was written and appeared in our local newspaper.

Soon after, I received a call from a booking agent from *The Today Show*. The article written on the poster contest and

Nick's ability to participate in everything he set his mind to, has caught their attention. Nick was invited to appear on the show, and we were ecstatic.

The words of his principal when the article from the poster contest was printed in the local newspaper rang through my mind. He said, "Mrs. S, this is going to lead to big things!"

I spoke with the booking agent several times and she scheduled videotaping at our home to have footage for Nick's story. A crew arrived at our home and spent the entire day filming. A few days before our appearance on the show, I received calls from several highly rated daytime talk shows, asking if we would be on their show the exact same day we were scheduled for *The Today Show*. I politely explained that we were already committed but would be happy to schedule with them at another time.

Well, let me tell you, that was a huge no-no. I did not realize how shows competed to see who could book whom first. I was told that if I did not take them up on their offer instead of the show I already committed to, they did not want us at all. I was so shocked, but not sorry. I kept the commitment; they had a wonderful surprise waiting for Nick— he would get to meet his sports idol.

The studio arranged a car to take us into New York with overnight accommodations in a beautiful hotel. Meghan and Nick were so excited to see the city.

After settling in our room, we took the elevator to the lobby and enjoyed a nice dinner in the hotel restaurant. Just as we finished eating, Nick took off in his wheelchair, telling us he'd be right back.

Michael and I just look at each other and shrugged, wondering where he was going. We watched as he rolled up to a few gentlemen sitting at the bar and started a conversation. After a few minutes, he returned to the table and asked Michael to take a picture of him and the gentleman.

It appeared as though Nick had recognized the new American Idol winner at the bar—and he graciously agreed to take a picture with Nick. The next morning, a car took us to Rockefeller Plaza. We were all a little nervous.

Once we arrived, a crew member escorted us to the "green room"; inside is a cozy waiting area with TVs broadcasting the live show. There was a wonderful spread of pastries and fruit for us to enjoy while we waited to be taken to the stage area.

As the producer attached the microphone to Nick, it dawned on him that he would be on TV any moment. He hastily asked Meghan to call his school, and when his principal answered, Nick very excitedly told him that he'd be going on any moment. To our complete surprise, the principal allowed the school to watch Nick on TV. The episode from *The Today Show* is on Nick's YouTube channel.

The airing of *The Today Show* has certainly brought quite a lot of attention to Nick; so much so that a company from South Korea contacted us to do a documentary. They wanted to fly a film crew to our home for a few days.

I could not imagine why they would travel so far and what this documentary would accomplish. Therefore, Michael and I questioned the producers extensively on the content they were looking for. It broke our hearts to discover that in some countries, children with deformities or disabilities are often put in orphanages or simply abandoned. The company's objective was to show Nick's capabilities and educate society that children with disabilities are not hopeless; that with love, understanding, and adaption they are valuable human beings and should be treated accordingly.

The documentary aired in South Korea and received great reviews. The company had called to arrange for another to be filmed. Several TV documentaries in the United States have also shown interest in Nick. My goodness, were going to be very busy!

CHAPTER FORTY

It was a beautiful, sunny 80-degree day with not a cloud in the sky.

We just enjoyed the Welcome Breakfast and it was time to head outside. The restaurant parking lot brimmed with motorcycles and riders put on their helmets and sunglasses or goggles as they started their bikes. The roar of the engines and the rumbling underfoot created an atmosphere of exhilaration.

Nick was the guest of honor for a benefit Motorcycle Run. A local club—with some amazing patrons—put together a memorial fund, and each year they chose a recipient. Nick was super excited to be on the lead bike, sitting snugly in the attached sidecar. He looked very cool as he slipped his shades on his face, which peeped out from under the helmet they provided for him to wear.

Two police cars started the procession, followed by a fire truck with blaring sirens. The lead bike—with Nick—was followed by almost two-hundred motorcycles.

Coordinated efforts by the police department guarded traffic lights and intersections allowed the entire procession of bikes an uninterrupted run to the designated location—a party waiting at the finish line.

Michael and I are at the very end of the procession in our truck, riding in the middle of the road. A police car followed to prevent cars from passing. We looked at each other with goofy smiles on our faces; it was an absolute thrill to look down the stretch of highway, with so many bikes as far as the eye could see—all for our little boy.

We drove down a dirt road clouded with dust. After a bend in the road, we saw a huge field set up with tents and tables. People have already gathered around Nick, who was celebrating along with his sisters, brother, cousins, and friends.

Live entertainment was set up on a stage and across the field was a rustic building where a huge amount of food was cooked and spread out in a mouthwatering buffet. To complete the feast, two decorated sheet cakes took center stage. They were decorated with Nick's picture and the names of all the sponsors.

But it didn't end there. He was also given a bright red Polaris four-wheeler, modified with a joystick. He was very surprised by this amazing gift; of course, he couldn't wait to take everyone for a ride.

CHAPTER FORTY-ONE

Nicks love for music did not end with the drums. I taught him to play the piano, and we ended up in the music store to buy him a harmonica. By the time we arrived home, he had already taught himself a song.

I preferred his singing, because he has an amazing voice—and I'm not being partial. Nick attended tryouts for both primetime singing programs, but he did not make the next round for either. , which broke his heart.

We believed that he sang really well, and he was invited to sing at a local music concert along with other guest musicians. He performed an original song, which was so beautiful, and the audience really connected with the words. It moved some folks to tears.

CHAPTER FORTY TWO

The Vine App is very popular. It's a six-second video that continues to loop repeatedly. It was on this application where Nick posted a Zombie prank that took place in a local department store.

Nick's friends used his cell phone to record a video as he rounded the corner with his face made up like a zombie, roaring horrifically; he scared an unsuspecting gentleman in the house ware aisle. The frightened man threw a large pack of paper towels at Nick.

This hilarious video went internationally viral and inspired them to film more zombie pranks. Fox International reached out to Nick to prank the lead actor from the *Walking Dead*, so Nick, Michael, and I were flown to Tokyo, Japan, where the prank took place.

Nick also had the opportunity to fly to California to collaborate with another famous prankster in filming *Chainsaw Massacre*.

133

Nick even appeared in a Vine documentary, and the movie *Natural Born Pranksters*. A variety of his Vine posts appeared on the TV show *Ridiculousness* and Nick Cannon's *Caught on Camera*.

Nick's pranks have unleashed opportunities and popularity. Now when people see Nick in public you hear "Hey, there's that guy from Vine".

His ability to entertain has drastically changed how society views him physically.

CHAPTER FORTY THREE

Nick was in High School and his self-perception has made a 180-degree turn around. My naturally happy child was not only dealing with the emotions of puberty, he felt the oppression of his peers.

He realized that he needed to make a positive change in his life and so he decided to join the JV Bowling Team. Although he was now part of a team, it did not fulfill the desire to change his self-esteem.

Michael and I knew we had to let him figure out this situation on his own. We honestly didn't know how to help him. Our words of encouragement and support were just not enough—until he informed us that he wanted to join the wrestling team. It was not uncommon for Nick to take us by surprise, but he really did it this time.

Our son, Mike, was a Varsity Wrestler in the same high school several years ago. Michael and I were very familiar with the demands this sport had on a body. Nick's right arm was very sensitive, and the bone was growing faster than the skin, causing him pain. If he hit his arm a certain way, chances are good the bone will come through the skin. But – of course—Nick had the answer to this dilemma; he insisted he wanted the right arm amputated.

That comment nauseated me, but Michael and I needed to carefully consider his request. My fear was that if we agreed to this type of surgery, the decision might come back to bite us in the ass.

We were at Nemours/Alfred I. DuPont hospital for children. Nick was in surgery for his arm amputation. To say we are nervous was the greatest understatement. One of the very best doctors in the country was performing the surgery. I could barely breathe waiting for Nick to be in recovery.

Just a few hours later, the doctor informed us the surgery was very successful. Nick would have a short stump with plenty of cushioning for physical activities.

He was in a lot of pain and pretty loopy from the pain medication. He insisted that he felt the pain in his arm—the arm he had before the surgery. It is ghost pain, and by the next day, he no longer had the sensation. We were given instructions for caring for his arm and took him home. He was extremely happy about the surgery but was bummed out he wouldn't be able to Trick or Treat; it was Halloween and he was stuck on the couch.

The auditorium was packed for Central's wrestling match. Nick was on the mat and the crowd cheered their support for him. His passion and zeal for life shone through and we had our happy kid back. Thank God, because it's been too long.

His sacrifice has paid off and he was a competitive athlete. An encounter with a parent after one of his wrestling matches has given him an epiphany. He had the answer to his "why"—why he was born this way, and what his life purpose was. He realized he was placed on this earth to make a difference.

Yes, you are, Nick. You have been doing that since the day you were born.

CHAPTER FORTY FOUR

It was nearing graduation, and the modifications to Nick's car were almost complete. After many hours of behind-the-wheel training, he was ready for his driving test.

We connected with a rehabilitation facility where a super-amazing rehab specialist had coordinated the state-mandated protocol towards Nick earning his driver's license. Several weeks later, Michael took Nick for his driving test.

I had no doubt Nick would pass his test, because he has amazing coordination, which I attribute to his self-discipline, determination, and can-do attitude.

Graduation day finally arrive! My baby, my last child was graduating high school.

He looked so handsome in his graduation gown. Nick's aide,—who has been by his side for the last four years,—had his relative cut and hem Nick's gown to size. His cap was decorated by his friends, adding a perfect finishing touch to the overall appearance.

138

We were seated outside on the huge lawn. It was sunny and very warm, but the weather couldn't warm me more than watching one of Nick's best friends carrying him up to the stage to receive his diploma. When he walked across the stage as his name was announced, the entire student body, teachers, and parents gave him a standing ovation. The thunderous cheers continue for at least a minute.

Michael and I were beyond emotional, smiling from ear to ear. We felt so blessed and proud, exactly how we felt for Marisa, Mike, and Meghan. I'm sure you can guess the tears were flowing.

Nick was accepted to the college of his choice which was located two states away. His best friend would also be attending and they planned to be roommates. A week before the first tuition payment was due, we had a round table discussion.

Nick was offered to be a cast member in an upcoming TV series. If he decided to accept, he had to move to California. I wanted him to pursue things that made him happy. Putting off college to fulfill a dream was a no-brainer to me. Opportunities in show business don't come often, but he could attend college any time.

Nick and I flew out to California and found a loft-style apartment he would share with a friend. We had just finished loading up his car, which we were shipping to Cali. Michael and I were very relieved that he wouldn't be living by himself—not that he couldn't. We spent years cultivating Nick's independence.

It was a tearful goodbye when we dropped him off at the airport,

Michael and I were so proud of the person Nick has become. I had all the faith in the world Nick would be okay, and relieved that I learned to Face Time.

CHAPTER FORTY-FIVE

OMG! I miss Nick so much. Our home is eerily quiet. There is no sudden burst of his laughter—which you could count each day; no "Mom, can you do this or that?" And no "Do you know where my [anything he can't find] is?" and no "See you later! I'm going out!"

As I scroll through my memories, I know it is an absolute miracle Michael and I have been blessed with four amazing children, and an even greater blessing that Nick beat the odds. I know without a doubt that he was placed with us to be loved unconditionally and raised in the same way as our other children. That was the pledge I made to GOD, so, if you ask me how we raised Nick or how we got through it, I will tell you that it was through pure love, faith in GOD, determination, and courage.

Oh and let us not forget: **It takes a village.**

A few months after he left for California, Nick called to inform us that the show had been cancelled and he was returning home.

In typical Nick fashion he used this experience as a stepping stone and quickly regrouped for his next project. With a plan in his mind and an unrelenting focus, he made the move to Tampa, which he now calls home. His plan: traveling the world and breaking the boundaries.

Thank you for reading Born to Break the Boundaries!

If you enjoyed this book, please feel free to leave a review at:

www.staceysantonastasso.com

To follow Nick Santonastasso on his amazing journey go to:

Instagram @nicksantonastasso

Facebook Nick Santonastasso

YouTube   Nick Santonastasso

Booknicksanto.com

About the Author

Stacey lives in New Jersey with her husband Michael. They have 4 grown children. G-Ma and Pop Pop to 8 amazing grandchildren. Although her faith has been strongly tested, she remains grounded in her Christian beliefs. Her passion is reading, shoes and cars. Encouraged by her youngest son Nick to write a book, about how he was raised, she took up the challenge to give hope to anyone who has the honor of raising a child.

ACKNOWLEDGEMENTS

Thank you, Nick, for planting the seed to write this book.

Carmela Guzzi for convincing me to write for other parents and not myself.

Eileen Sakevich for all the many hours cheering me on and your awesome computer skills.

My co-workers, Sue Kaiser, Jane Walling, Kathy Torres, Claudia Ganopoulos and Lori Burdge-Marzarella, thank you for believing I could actually accomplish writing a book.

Carolyn Colleen my mentor and mostly importantly my FIERCE friend.

To my Village – I'm so grateful God placed you in our lives.

And last, but not least, thank you Michael for your love, support, and the emotional rollercoaster re-lived to create this book.

Made in the USA
Middletown, DE
23 April 2019